Woman Poet

Woman Poet

WOMEN-IN-LITERATURE, INCORPORATED

Reno 1985

WOMEN-IN-LITERATURE, INCORPORATED

P.O. Box 60550, Reno, Nevada 89506

Cover photo of Lisel Mueller by Alan Plog

Acknowledgements: "Hospital" by Ardyth Bradley, *Banyan Anthology*; "Hearth" and "This Is How Memory Works" by Patricia Hampl, *Resort and Other Poems* (Houghton Mifflin); "When My Father Waters His Trees" by Linda Hasselstrom, *Sez*; "The First Day of Summer," "On the Northwest Hiawatha," and a previous version of "Visitors" by Kathleen Norris, *The Middle of the World* (University of Pittsburgh Press); "In the Field, Treasure" by Anita Skeen, *Continental Drift*; "A Light in the Doorway" by Cary Waterman, *The Salamander Migration* (University of Pittsburgh Press). For Judith Minty: "Breathing in the Woods," *Poetry Now*; "Country Road in October," *Hawaii Review*; "Meeting My Father at the River," *Passages North*; and "Walking," *The Barat Review* and *Mickle Street Review*. For Lisel Mueller: "About Suffering They Were Never Wrong," *New Letters*; "After Whistler," *The Brockport Forum*; "Bread and Apples," *Tendril*; "Chances Are," *Oyez Review*; "Crossing Over," *American Poetry Review*; "Fugitive," *Poetry*; "Monet Refuses the Operation," *Paris Review*; "The Triumph of Life: Mary Shelley," *The Need to Hold Still* (Louisiana State University Press); and "Your Tired, Your Poor," *Chicago Review*.

Due to the tardiness in our publication date, some of the material in this anthology has been previously published; we have given the permissions needed for this.

Library of Congress Cataloging in Publication Data
(Revised for Vol. 3)

Main entry under title:

Woman Poet.

  Contents: v. 1. The West—v. 2. The East—v. 3. The Midwest.
  1. American poetry—Women authors.   2. American poetry—
20th century.   3. American poetry—Women authors—History
and criticism—Addresses, essays, lectures.   I. Women-in-
Literature, Incorporated (U.S.)
PS589.W57   811′.54′0809287   81-69793
ISBN 0-935634-01-0 (v. 1)   AACR2
ISBN 0-935634-00-2 (pbk.: v. 1)

International Standard Book Number: 0-935634-04-5 (paper)
                                    0-935634-05-3 (hardcover)
International Standard Serial Number: 0195-6183

Manufactured in the United States of America

FIRST EDITION

This publication has been made possible, in part, through grants
from the American Association of University Women and from
the National Endowment for the Arts through the Nevada State
Council on the Arts. We thank them for their support.

Woman Poet

Editor-in-Chief	Elaine Dallman
Guest Editor	Martha Friedberg
Special Editorial Advisors	Laurel Neesan
	Catharine Stimpson
Editorial Board	Ruth Bevans
	Terralin Carroll
	Joyce Cohen
	Lynda Ingelhart
	Dorothy Kline
	Sandra Macias
	Adrianne Marcus
	Lisa Sheretz
	Shirley Sousa
Editorial Assistants	Virginia Kristensen
	Terry Parrish
Marketing/Distribution	Ruth Bevans
	Adela Bishop
	Charlene Eley
	Marcia Freedman
	(Israel)
	JoAn Johnstone
	Shelley Lescott
	Mary Ann McFadden
	Susanne Muller
	(Switzerland)
	Marvin Picollo School
	(Reno, Nevada)
	Retired Senior Volunteer
	Program
	(Reno, Nevada)
	Frances Walker
	Women-in-Literature
	Networking Audience
	(Chicago) and
	Leah Theodore,
	WILNA Coordinator
	(Chicago)

Editorial Correspondence
Elaine Dallman, *Woman Poet*,
P.O. Box 60550, Reno, Nevada 89506

Submissions
Elaine Dallman, Editor-in-Chief,
P.O. Box 60550, Reno, Nevada 89506

We welcome unsolicited submissions by writers. Work must be original and unpublished in any version. We reserve the right to reprint. Work which would appear simultaneously in our anthology and an author's collection will be considered if crediting of *Woman Poet* is possible.

We wish we could read all manuscripts in one day's turnaround. We apologize that we cannot. Please allow a minimum of eight weeks for our volunteer editorial staff to carefully read your manuscript. Delays imply no disrespect for the work submitted but reflect the limitations imposed by too heavy a workload.

If work is to be returned, it must be accompanied by a self-addressed envelope with sufficient postage.

Publisher
Women-in-Literature, Incorporated, a non-profit publisher, P.O. Box 60550, Reno, Nevada 89506.

Subscriptions
Subscriptions or 4 volume sets beginning with any designated volume, U.S.A., Canada, or Mexico: Institutions $38.00, individuals $30.00, students $27.00. Other countries add $3.00 for each volume for delivery.

Classroom Discount Rates
Please write for special classroom discount rates. Free teacher's subscription with classroom adoption.

Payment
Nevada residents add 6% sales tax.

Checks should be payable to *Woman Poet*, P.O. Box 60550, Reno, Nevada 89506.

Advertising Rates
Correspondence about advertising inserts should be addressed to *Woman Poet*, Department A, P.O. Box 60550, Reno, Nevada 89506.

Change of Address
Please notify the press and local postmaster immediately, providing *both* the old and the new address. *Allow 6 weeks for change.* Claims for missing volumes should be made within one month of publication. The publishers will supply missing volumes free only when losses have been sustained in transit and reserve stock will permit.

Woman Poet

VOLUME III

The Midwest

Staff Note

Photo by Chip Miller

Martha Friedberg (Guest Editor)

Martha Friedberg began moving in poetry circles in 1961 when she became a student of poet John Logan. Since then her poetic involvements have included:

- co-founder of The Poetry Center with a group of poets and writers in 1974;
- a member of the selection committee for Ragdale, a residential center for writers and artists in Lake Forest, Illinois;
- a trustee of the Modern Poetry Association;
- publication of her chapbook *Finally* (Vixen Press), with wood engravings, design, printing, and binding by artist Caryl Seidenberg.

Friedberg was born, raised, and married in Chicago. She brought up her children there, and she continues to live and work in Chicago.

Preface

BY CARY WATERMAN

A current belief held about contemporary poetry written by women is that it deals for the most part with certain heretofore unmentionable or uninteresting subjects. Like babies. Or grandmothers. Or gardens. It is curious that first we had to emancipate just such subjects (previously thought to be too light-weight for serious poetry) only to have them become what is now considered the be-all and end-all for women writers. Well, let the reader prepare. There are poems in this anthology about virtually *everything*, from cosmic explosions to shoplifting, from death to murder to sex. But (and this is a big but) there is a common ground to the poems contained herein. There is a certain latitude, a definition of space, and a reach.

This anthology is the third in a regional series brought out by WOMAN POET. In this, the Midwest volume, writers from virtually all the Midwestern states are represented. There are some hybrids, that is women who grew up in the Midwest but have since been on the move, or women who have immigrated to the Midwest from other parts of the country. These women, as serious writers, share certain convictions. One is to settle for no less than the truth. Another, practiced even by literary beginners, is to refuse to apologize for themselves or go bowing and scraping from the room called poetry. They are concerned with real things, as Anita Skeen says in her poem "In the Field, Treasure":

> She was a lover of primary sources:
> rock, wheat, bone . . .

There has been much talk about "regionalism" in literature recently. I do not believe that the deep, recurring themes of poetry are particular to region. The landscape of the poem may present us with many different styles and scenes. But the concerns remain the same. And they remain the same not only from region to region, or country to country, but also across time. I have been referred to as a Midwestern poet although I was born in Connecticut and spent the impressionable years (both visually and spiritually) of my childhood there. Now I find Connecticut in Minnesota and an ocean in the crackly fields of fall corn. However, poets need gatherings, and whether those gatherings be regional or not, in print or in public, they are necessary and anticipated.

The Midwest, which has in some way penetrated the vision of all of these writers, can be harsh to an extreme. When I think of this part of the country where I have lived now for fifteen years, certain symbols come to mind: one of them is the character of Beret in O. E. Rölvaag's *Giants in the Earth*, who goes mad faced by the desolation of a Midwestern winter; another one is the tornado, that unpredictable and murderous act of nature. There is in some of these poems a harshness in voice or landscape; and there is also the harshness that comes from stretching the artful muscles which had atrophied for centuries. Virginia Woolf in *A Room of One's Own* says:

> All these minutely obscure lives remain to be recorded, I said . . . and went on in thought through the streets of London feeling in imagination the pressure of dumbness, the accumulation of unrecorded life.

Of course harshness, which sometimes goes masked as self-revelation or bare honesty, is not enough to hold us. It is not enough to be angry at the world. It is finally not enough to rage at the culture that permitted the lives of our grandmothers to go unrecorded. There is more and we find it in the best of these poems. They have a compassion to them, a loving of the toughness of realities, and an acceptance of the life Neruda referred to as "a necessary obligation."

These are poems of transformation. From birth to death to birth. About changes in love and resignation and independence. There is no time for despair. We have claimed the body and the mind, the gray memories of our ancestors and the blue water of our own dreams. We are not seeking separation or even equality as it is understood in the culture today.

Rather we seek for a better place to write poems, have children and love both men and women. These poems show the way, point to the beginnings of that time, the place Lisel Mueller describes in her poem "Chances Are":

> . . . She imagines
> a magic country . . .
> at the bottom of the world
> where even barren women
> give birth, a five-pound body
> that bears the weight of the earth,
> the breath that keeps it turning.

Lisel Mueller

LAKE FOREST, ILLINOIS

Photo by Jenny Mueller

The Triumph of Life: Mary Shelley

The voice addressing us is that of Mary Wollstonecraft Shelley, 1796–1851, daughter of the radical philosopher William Godwin and the feminist Mary Wollstonecraft, who died as a result of her birth. She eloped with Percy Shelley, who was married to Harriet Westbrook at the time, and became his second wife after Harriet committed suicide. Shelley and Mary lived a nomadic life, moving around England and the Continent, never settling down anywhere for long. Three of their four children died in infancy. Their eight years together were a series of crises, many of them brought about by Shelley's restlessness and the drain of outsiders on their emotional and physical resources. After Shelley's accidental drowning, Mary, who was twenty-four at the time of his death, supported herself and their surviving son by her own writing and by editing and annotating Shelley's work. She published the first complete edition of his poems. Her own works consist of essays, short stories, and six novels, of which *Frankenstein*, written when she was nineteen, is the most famous. Her journal has been an important biographical source for Shelley's and her life together.

1

My father taught me to think
to value mind over body,
to refuse even the airiest cage

to be a mouth as well as an ear,
to ask difficult questions,
not to marry because I was asked,
not to believe in heaven

None of this kept me from bearing
four children and losing three
by the time I was twenty-two

He wanted to think I sprang
from his head like the Greek goddess

He forgot that my mother died
of my birth, *The Rights of Women*
washed away in puerperal blood
and that I was her daughter too

2

I met him when I was sixteen
He came to sit at my father's feet
and stayed to sit at mine

We became lovers
who remained friends
even after we married

A marriage of true minds
It is what you want
It is what we wanted

We did not believe in power
We were gentle
We shared our bodies with others
We thought we were truly free

My father taught us there was a solution
to everything, even evil

We were generous, honest
We thought we had the solution

and still, a woman walked
into the water because of us

3

After that death I stopped
believing in solutions

And when my children died
it was hard not to suspect
there was a god, a judgment

For months I wanted to be
with those three small bodies,
to be still in a dark place

No more mountain passes
No more flight from creditors
with arms as long as our bills

No more games to find out
who was the cleverest of us all

No more ghost stories by the fire
with my own ghosts at the window,
smiles sharpened like sickles
on the cold stone of the moon

For months I made a fortress
of my despair
"A defect of temper," they called it
His biographers never liked me

You would have called it a sickness,
given me capsules and doctors,
brushes and bright paints,
kits for paper flowers

4
An idea whose time has come,
you say about your freedom
but you forget the reason

Shall I remind you of history,
of choice and chance, the wish and the world,
of courage and locked doors,
biology and fate?

I wanted what you want,
what you have

If I could have chosen my children
and seen them survive
I might have believed in equality,
written your manifestos

Almost two hundred years
of medical science divide us

5
And yet, my father was right
It was the spirit that won in the end

After the sea had done
what it could to his flesh
I knew he was my husband
only by the books
in his pockets: Sophocles, Keats

The word survives the body

It was then I decided
not to marry again
but to live for the word

6
I allowed his body to be burned
on that Italian beach
Rome received his ashes

You have read that our friend
snatched his heart from the fire
You call it a grisly act,
something out of my novel

You don't speak of the heart
in your letters, your sharp-eyed poems
You speak about your bodies
as though they had no mystery,
no caves, no sudden turnings

You claim isolation, night-sweats,
hanging on by your teeth

You don't trust the heart
though you define death
as the absence of heartbeat

You would have taken a ring,
a strand of hair, a shoelace
—a symbol, a souvenir

not the center, the real thing

7
*He died
and the world gave no outward sign*

I started a Journal of Sorrow

But there were the words, the poems,
passion and ink spilling
over the edges of all those sheets
There was the hungry survivor
of our bodily life together

Would it have lasted, our marriage,
if he had stayed alive?

As it was, we fed each other
like a pair of thrushes
I gave his words to the world
and they came back to me
as bread and meat and apples,
art and nature, mind and flesh
keeping each other alive

His last, unfinished poem
was called *The Triumph of Life*

8

You are surprised at my vision,
that a nineteen-year-old girl
could have written that novel,
how much I must have known

But I only wanted to write
a tale to tremble by,
what is oddly called a romance

By accident I slid
out of my century
into yours of white-coated men
in underground installations,
who invent their own destruction
under fluorescent lights

And in a few more decades,
when your test-tube babies sprout,
you will call me the prophet
of ultimate horror again

It was only a private nightmare
that dreamed the arrogance of your time

I was not your Cassandra
In any age, life has to be lived
before we can know what it is

Voyager

For my father, 1897–1976

No one's body could be that light,
not even after it burns—
I know this is not you,
has nothing to do with you

I know you stand on a ship
looking through the eyeholes,
near-sighted and patient as always,
still knowing everything

No matter what language they speak,
the boatmen in the black barges
that pass you, you will answer

No matter what bundle of time
they inhabit, you will direct them,
warn them once more and once more in vain

You who changed countries more often than shoes
can step ashore anywhere;
loneliness is the anchor
you've always carried with you

The desert is what I would have spared you,
the wilderness after my mother died,
your fixed star

Everything could be borne,
all knowledge, all separation
except that final one

Slowly you turned to stone

And I, your daughter/keeper—
what did I know about
the sentience of stone?
I watered you with indignities
and tears, but you never bloomed

Now both of you have entered
the history of your photographs;
together, young and smiling,
you stand on the steps of Notre Dame

"These are my parents, friends and children,"
I say, but it is hopeless

I want the impossible photograph,
one that would show the world
your trick, how you and she

pulled joy from any borrowed hat
or sleeve, a survivor's art

This is the hardest knowledge;
that no one will remember you
when your daughters are gone

Five years before you died
I took your picture;
you were wearing a dark jacket
and your hair was white

Now I hold the negative
up to the light and the sun streams through

Bread and Apples

In the tale
the apple tree rises before her,
not in an orchard,
but solitary and sudden
in a world she does not know
is supernatural. It asks
in an old woman's voice
to be relieved of its red-cheeked burden.
Further on, in a field,
she hears the terrified cries
of bread almost burned in its fireplace.
She does not ask who made bread
in an uninhabited wilderness.

So memory raises landmarks,
unbidden, out of place
and time. My father sits
in the long-discarded chair;
the pages of the history book
he leafs through keep springing back
to the beginning. He does not explain
his presence here. Without a question
I pull the bread from the ashes
and place it on the ground to cool.

Midnight

The spirits are not fooled
by my faked sleep, my regular breathing;

as though it were Notre Dame again,
the rose window

You are changed, you wear
the pale clothes of summer,
your skin and hair are black

How can you see? Your glasses
are whitewashed and there are holes
where your teeth used to be

Nevertheless you smile at me
across an enormous distance,
as you have so many times,
to let me know you have arrived

the magic animations
do not take place. I wait
for the window to tear off its bandages,
cured of its blindness,
the tape recorder to fall in love
with its new blue voice,
the leggy shadows on the floor
to pick each other up and start dancing.
But only the photographs in my head
relent: tonight it is
my grandfather's small-boned figure
with its white mustache
standing on a boardwalk
in Europe, calling me back.
He waves as if it were easy,
as if it were now or never
that the sea between us
would part for my long walk home.

Your Tired, Your Poor

ASYLUM

I cannot ask you to paint the tops
of your bare mountains green
or gentle your coasts to lessen
my homesickness. Beggar, not chooser,
I hand you the life you say I must leave
at the border, bundled and tied.
You riffle through it without looking,
stamp it and put it out the back
for the trash collector. "Next," you call.

I am free. I stand in the desert,
heavy with what I smuggled in
behind my eyes and under my tongue:
memory and language, my rod and staff,
my leper's rattle, my yellow star.

ENGLISH AS A SECOND LANGUAGE

The underpaid young teacher
prints the letters t, r, e, e
on the blackboard and imagines
forests and gardens springing up
in the tired heads of her students.

But they see only four letters;
a vertical beam weighed down
by a crushing crossbar
and followed by a hook,
and after the hook, two squiggles,
arcane identical twins
which could be spying eyes
or ready fists, could be handles,
could be curled seedlings, could take root,
could develop leaves.

CROSSING OVER

There comes a day when the trees
refuse to let you pass
until you name them. Stones
speak up and reveal themselves
as the poor of your new country.
Then you see that the moon
has chosen to follow you here,
and find yourself humming the music
you stuffed your ears against.
You dream in rhyme, in a language
you never wanted to understand.
When you pick up the telephone,
the voices from home arrive
sighing, bent by the ocean.
Their letters bear postage stamps
that surprise you with their bright, flat birds.

Chances Are

"100 schoolchildren murdered by Bokassa I in Central
African Empire."

"Uterus removed, New Zealand woman gives birth to
healthy daughter."

Newspaper headlines on facing pages

Hope is a fat seed pod,
skin stretched tight around it,
ready to burst. When it does,
the ancient crier calls
the light year of the child.

Every few seconds they arrive,
shot into time and space,
their mouths remembering
the shape of buds. In Ohio
a woman diminishing to a stalk
in a white bed picks up
the newspaper and reads
about one hundred children
massacred by their government.
Dismisses it. She skips
to a story she can believe
in the presence of her child's
soft, rhythmic tugs. She imagines
a magic country of sheep
at the bottom of the world,
where even barren women
give birth; a five-pound body
bearing the weight of the earth;
the breath that keeps it turning.

Widow

What the neighbors bring to her kitchen
is food for the living. She wants to eat
the food of the dead, their pure
narcotic of dry, black seeds.
Why, without him, should she desire
the endurance offered by meat and grain,
the sugars that glue the soul to the body?
She thanks them, but does not eat,
consumes strong coffee as if it were air
and she the vigilant candle

on a famous grave, until the familiar
sounds of the house become strange,
turn into messages in the new language
he has been forced to learn.
All night she works on the code,
almost happy, her body rising
like bread, while the food in its china caskets
dries out on the table.

After the Face Lift

The woman who used to be my age
is shopping for endive and bell-shaped peppers.
Her face has retracted sleepless nights,
denies any knowledge of pain.
The black eyes given her
by the death of someone she loved
are gone. I look at her,
wondering how it feels to remember,
under the skin of a thirty-year old,
something that happened at forty.
I wonder if she excites her husband
in her new half-strangeness
or has betrayed him, removed
their years together like the soiled
part of a roller towel
yanked in the wrong direction.
Her unused face reveals nothing.
She moves ahead, her cart
piled high with greens, and reaches
for a bunch of jonquils, this year's first
yellow, about to open.

Fugitive

My life is running away with me;
the two of us are in cahoots.
I hold still while it paints
dark circles under my eyes,
streaks my hair gray, stuffs pillows
under my dress. In each new room
the mirror reassures me
I'll not be recognized.
I'm learning to travel light,
like the juice in the power line.
My baggage, swallowed by memory,

weighs almost nothing. No one suspects
its value. When they knock on my door,
badges flashing, I open up:
I don't match their description.
Wrong room, they say, and apologize.
My life in the corner winks
and wipes off my fingerprints.

About Suffering
They Were Never Wrong

They could have told us that the particulars,
those tiny chips, would remain embedded
in the mind she took with her,
the woman down the block
who hanged herself,

and that her mind was not like her house
with its open door, its yard full of flowers,

that even the cleanest floor
does not hide the absolute dropoff,
and when we walked past her windows,
thinking we looked into a room,
we looked at smoked glass and our own reflection.

How well they understood
that the lives of other people
are as full of secrets
as the lives of spies,
who give up the trivial ones
to appease the neighbors,

and that the real one
implodes one sunny afternoon
in October, a day so mild
the roses are tricked into blooming again.

After Whistler

There are girls who should have been swans.
At birth their feathers are burned;
their human skins never fit.
When the other children
line up on the side of the sun,
they will choose the moon,

that precious aberration.
They are the daughters mothers
worry about. All summer,
dressed in gauze, they flicker
inside the shaded house,
drawn to the mirror, where their eyes,
blue, languid moths, hang dreaming.
It's winter they wait for, the first snowfall
with the steady interior hum
only they can hear;
they stretch their arms, as if they were wounded,
toward the bandages of snow.
Briefly, the world is theirs
in its perfect frailty.

Up North

Already they are flying back,
gray clumps with nervous wings,
always the first to know.

Otherwise, mere inklings.
An occasional fiery branch
flags us down from the green,
but the leaves still rub soft-skinned
against each other, and the tomatoes
dawdle as though red
were a suitor willing to wait.
The trunks of the birches are lit
from within, like ideal nudes
who have no season. We lie
body to body under the trees
as we did last summer. Nothing has changed.
I search your face for the year,
but my eyes have aged at the same rate
and I've learned nothing. Plums
on the table beside us hoard
their juice inside sealed barrels
of gleaming skin, but you and I
don't hoard our sweetness, hoard anything.

Monet Refuses the Operation

Doctor, you say there are no haloes
around the streetlights in Paris
and what I see is an aberration
caused by old age, an affliction.
I tell you it has taken me all my life
to arrive at the vision of gas lamps as angels,
to soften and blur and finally banish
the edges you regret I don't see,
to learn that the line I called the horizon
does not exist and sky and water,
so long apart, are the same state of being.
Fifty-four years before I could see
Rouen cathedral is built
of parallel shafts of sun,
and now you want to restore
my youthful errors: fixed
notions of top and bottom,
the illusion of three-dimensional space,
wisteria separate
from the bridge it covers.
What can I say to convince you
the Houses of Parliament dissolve
night after night to become
the fluid dream of the Thames?
I will not return to a universe
of objects that don't know each other,
as if islands were not the lost children
of one great continent. The world
is flux, and light becomes what it touches,
becomes water, lilies on water,
above and below water,
becomes lilac and mauve and yellow
and white and cerulean lamps,
small fists passing sunlight
so quickly to one another
that it would take long, streaming hair
inside my brush to catch it.
To paint the speed of light!
Our weighted shapes, these verticals,
burn to mix with air
and change our bones, skin, clothes
to gases. Doctor,
if only you could see
how heaven pulls earth into its arms
and how infinitely the heart expands
to claim this world, blue vapor without end.

Lisel Mueller: Biography

BY ARDYTH BRADLEY

"HISTORY PLAYED ME FALSE," Lisel Mueller says in one of her poems. This is not a complaint about the disruptions inherent in being born a German in the first third of the 20th century. It expresses, rather, her perplexity at the string of events that removed her from Nazi Germany and so saved her from the destruction that country inflicted and suffered. To those who know her, it all seems like an inevitability—her destiny being inseparable from her character. But Lisel herself takes a much more uncertain view of the history that brought her to America, that led her to her happy marriage, that drew from her her poems.

This history begins with Lisel's father. Fritz Carl Neumann, the son of conservative, middle-class German parents, wrote his doctoral dissertation (on Ibsen) in the trenches of World War I. During the war and the years immediately following, he underwent a conversion to—or, rather, a progressively more serious involvement with—the political left. In the 1920's he taught in Hamburg at the Lichtwarkschule, an educationally progressive and politically liberal secondary school. In the evenings he gave political lectures to adults. He was, for a time, as he said in his memoirs, a "fellow traveler" of the Communists. Hitler came to power in January 1933. By Easter the Hamburg school system had dismissed Dr. Neumann.

For a while he was employed by several Jewish families to teach their children privately (since public schools had been made increasingly unbearable for Jews). There were a few other short-term jobs in Germany. But it was clear, particularly after the three days he was held by the Gestapo on suspicion of subversion, that Germany was not a place he could safely remain, even if it were possible for him to support himself and his wife and two daughters there. Dr. Neumann's solitary exile took him to various teaching jobs in France, Italy, England, and, finally, the United States.

During the six years of forced separation from her husband, Lisel's mother, Ilse Neumann, supported herself and her daughters by teaching in an elementary school in Hamburg. She and her husband were unchanged in their devotion to each other and their opposition to all that Hitler stood for. Lisel, too, understood her father's absence, was proud of him, and knew she mustn't discuss him with schoolmates.

Finally, in June 1939, Lisel's mother, Lisel, and her sister, Inge, were able to join Dr. Neumann in the United States. Lisel was 15. Suffering terribly from homesickness, she was unhappy for about a year. Now she says that 15 was the best age of all to switch countries: "At fifteen you want more than anything to be accepted, assimilated into the environment around you."

And, for a poet—whether or not she knows at 15 that she is one—this is a good age for making the transition from one language to another. Lisel was placed in the senior class of an Evansville (Indiana) high school. She had studied English in Germany, and now she rapidly added to her vocabulary. English metaphor, however, remained a puzzle to her for some time, and consequently she was unimpressed by the poets studied in her high school literature courses.

But one poet not taught in her school was just what she needed at the time. This was Carl Sandburg, whose plain diction seemed to Lisel exotic as well as easy. This was her first encounter with modern poetry in any language. Under the influence of Sandburg and "adolescent loneliness," she began to write poems.

At 16 Lisel entered Evansville College (where her father was teaching) as a pre-med student. She was attracted to medicine not by any particular scientific bent but out of an idealistic desire to cure people. Her worst grades were in her major subjects, and she could never see through the microscope what she was supposed to see. After a year, still guided by youthful idealism, she changed her major to sociology.

Lisel's minor at Evansville College was Speech. She had dreams of a career in theatre or radio—acting, writing, or directing. She did, as a matter of fact, write two scripts for the local radio station: a documentary on Keats and a dramatization of Maupassant's "The Necklace." And during her college years she was still writing poems "as some people write passionate letters they do not mail." But, she says, it never occurred to her to become a *writer*, and soon she stopped writing altogether. "'Life' took over: marriage, jobs, graduate school, friends."

Lisel met Paul Mueller in December 1941. Paul was a literature student (and later a music student) at Evansville College. He was drafted in January 1943. In June 1943 he got a three-day furlough, and Lisel and he married. At the end of the furlough, he was shipped to the Aleutians. Lisel stayed on in Evansville, graduated in June 1944, and worked that summer as a social worker. In August Paul was stationed in Spokane, Washington, and Lisel joined him there in the married soldiers' housing, officially called Victory Heights and unofficially labeled Poverty Flats. Lisel worked in a nursery school for the six months she and Paul had together before he was shipped to Okinawa. She returned then to her parents—this time in Winnetka, Illinois, where they taught at the North Shore Country Day School. Again Lisel worked in a nursery school.

Following his discharge from the army in 1946, Paul Mueller entered Roosevelt University in Chicago and, following his graduation in 1948, Indiana University. Lisel worked at a succession of jobs. She was a case worker for the American Red Cross and the Bloomington, Indiana, juvenile court. She worked once again in a nursery school, and at the public library in Bloomington. And all those years, she says, there were no poems.

But there was something that anyone who knows Lisel's poetry will find significant. She studied folklore under Stith Thompson. In the first graduate department in folklore in the country, she found what she calls "the treasure mountain of metaphor," which gives so many deep, human themes to her poems. She says, "The great fairy tales are not mere entertainments; they signify. Their actions are metaphors for the crises every human life must go through. The characters are us at the threshold of adolescence and, by extension, of any difficult and meaningful change."

In 1953 Paul received his Ph.D. in musicology. Another event occurred that year which, according to Lisel, started her real apprenticeship as a poet.

"In 1953 my mother died. Whenever someone asks me the inevitable question 'What made you become a poet?' I remember a calm, sunny afternoon a few weeks after her death, when I sat in a lovely backyard in Evanston, Illinois, and felt an immense need to put some of what I felt about her death and that particular afternoon into a poem: to 'say' my feelings, vent them, put them into some order, some context I could understand. If the impulse was therapeutic, it was also the start of my 'real' writing. I was 29, and it was the first poem I had written in about eight years. After that small, awkward poem, so hard to write, I knew I never wanted to stop making poems again."

In 1953 there were no poetry workshops for someone like Lisel. So she began on her own—reading and writing and throwing a lot into the wastebasket.

Nevertheless, within a fairly short time, she was having poems printed in such periodicals as *The New Yorker*, *Poetry*, *Sewanee Review*, and *Nation*.

Lisel's first daughter was born in 1957, and another came in 1962. Lisel has written (in her monograph *Learning to Play by Ear*) about the circumstances that helped to keep her making poems during the beginning years of writing and especially the beginning years of motherhood. They included a group of poet friends who met regularly. Also, Lisel was the poetry reviewer for *The Chicago Daily News*. This meant that she was reading and thinking about most of the poetry being published.

And there was (and is) her husband. Lisel and Paul Mueller have practiced in their marriage and in parenthood a degree of cooperation that remains rare. In addition, what Lisel has called her "education"—her reading of poetry and poetic theory during her first writing years—was undertaken jointly with Paul, who continues to be her most important critic. Close family ties—with her parents and sister as well as with her husband and children—have been an integrating force in her life and writing.

Lisel's first book, *Dependencies* (University of North Carolina Press), was published in 1965. Next, *Life of a Queen* (a chapbook) was published by Juniper Press in 1970. *The Private Life*, published by Louisiana State University Press, was the Lamont Poetry Selection in 1975, the first year that the Academy of American Poets began awarding the Lamont prize for a poet's second book. In 1977 Juniper Press issued the second chapbook, *Voices from the Forest*; and, in 1980, Two Hands Press published *Learning to Play by Ear*, on her apprenticeship as a writer.

Lisel's most recent books are *The Need to Hold Still* (LSU, 1980), a collection of poems which won the 1981 American Book Award, and two volumes of translation, *Selected Later Poems of Marie Luise Kaschnitz* (Princeton, 1980) and *Whether or Not* (Juniper, 1984). She has completed the manuscript for a new collection, *Second Language*. All of Lisel Mueller's poems in this *Woman Poet—The Midwest* volume are from this newest manuscript, except for the Mary Shelley poem.

Lisel's poems have appeared in such anthologies as *The Contemporary American Poets* (ed. Strand), *The New Yorker Book of Poems*, *The Poetry Anthology, 1912–1977* (eds. Hine and Parisi), *New Poems by American Poets, 2* (ed. Humphries), *The Pushcart Prize, II: Best of the Small Presses, Heartland* (ed. Stryk), *Rising Tides: 20th Century Women Poets*, and many others, including textbooks and the three-poet anthology *Voyages to the Inland Sea*, I.

She has had critical essays published in *Poetry, Ploughshares, New, Shenandoah*, and other journals. She was the co-translator of a stage version of Hugo von Hofmannsthal's verse play *Das Salzburger Grosse Welttheater*, which was performed at the Goodman Theater in Chicago.

Lisel has taught poetry writing on various campuses, including Elmhurst College, Goddard College, Wichita State University, Washington University, and the University of Chicago. She also has served on the staff of a number of writers' conferences. She currently teaches in the Warren Wilson MFA Program for Writers and is a contributing editor to *Tendril*.

Reading the memoirs of Lisel's father recently, I was struck with how much this European intellectual was a formed, whole *mind* in a way that our unjoined beliefs and desires, our reflexive ironies, hardly let us be. I find something of that same integrity in his daughter. In an era which has emphasized the ugly truth beneath a surface ideality, Lisel Mueller has created through her life some of the ideal reality of the intellectual tradition out of which she came. Reticent about whatever she has suffered through the disintegrations of this century, she accepts with wonder the circumstances in which she has kept whole (as expressed in these lines from "On Reading an Anthology of Postwar German Poetry," *The Private Life*):

> I know enough to refuse to say
> that life is good,
> but I act as though it were.
> And skeptical about love, I survive
> by the witness of my own.

 ARDYTH BRADLEY has written critical essays—on such diverse topics as the poetry of Wallace Stevens and the sculpture of Barbara Hepworth— in *Twentieth Century Literature, The Chicago Daily News, Helicon Nine*, and *Open Places*.

Lisel Mueller, Voyager and Visionary

BY ROBERTA SIMONE

IN THE POETRY of Lisel Mueller from 1965 to the present, one sees the progression of a growing, journeying mind absorbing and communicating what it has learned through experiences and focusing and refocusing its vision as it moves closer to its object: the end of life, the meaning of life. As Mary Shelley says in "The Triumph of Life,"

> In any age, life has to be lived
> Before we can know what it is.

Lisel Mueller has been like a tour guide who, though new herself to the sites, is well aware of the historical significance and interprets aloud each turn, each new landscape, and each monument. None of us will take the exact trip, but we will all take one like it.

Lisel Mueller said in her first published volume, *Dependencies* (1965), "I write about experiences . . . that I believe to be natural landmarks in the course of living for everyone . . . . I am primarily driven by a perception of life as process." The metaphor of journey is pervasive in her poetry, but not merely in the sense of starting at a particular place and ending at another. Rather, it begins with a coming to awareness and a continual moving, sometimes forwards, sometimes backwards, sometimes sideways, occasionally standing still briefly in the dark or in a haze, to see a flash of light. In "A Grackle Observed" (*Dependencies*, 1965), the bird suddenly appears and suddenly disappears, leaving only the "shining part / of himself behind / as though / brightness must / . . . enter the mind outright / as vision, as pure light." The mind is like a camera, storing visions and insights, just as photographs are frozen seconds of history which tourists collect and store in albums. So the photograph, the film, and the pre-

technological "photograph," the painting, are metaphors that recur in Mueller's poems, recording her own journey through life.

It is not surprising that journeying should be at the center of her poetry: her father, a professor of history, "changed countries more often than shoes" (a quotation from Bertolt Brecht about the fate of emigrés, in "Voyager"), and she, herself, was an immigrant to the United States at age 15. Immigration, especially when it necessitates the learning of a new language, makes the new arrival particularly aware of translation in addition to transition. The *word* becomes more significant to one who must be bilingual, one for whom there is not only newness of landscape, of detail, of culture, but also, perforce, a new way to hear and express what one sees. A new code must be broken and mastered in order to survive. Eventually it becomes a key to the insight that only the scenery has changed: the characters, the theme, the plot of the play remain the same—human lives being lived with the same mystery at the heart, the same tensions of birth and death, love and violence, water and sky, sun and moon.

Lisel Mueller's poems in this anthology, all new (with the exception of "The Triumph of Life," which was published in *Voices from the Forest*, 1977) and to be published in her forthcoming volume, aptly entitled *Second Language*, continue the metaphors of travel and transition and of history—keeping records through words and graphic representations.

In "Your Tired, Your Poor" the beggar/exile/Jew comes to a new land, probably the United States, that accepts him, if unfeelingly, and the immigrant, who can smuggle from his old life only memories, slowly, confusedly begins to adapt. The hardest part, like being suspended in nowhere, occurs when, while the new life is still a puzzle, the old life startles because it is no longer familiar: the "voices from home arrive / sighing," the mail bears "postage stamps / that surprise you . . . ." In school, the letters of the new alphabet are meaningless, then frightening, scratches: the consonants look like the old instruments of torture and pain from which the exile has fled (*t* and *r* like "cross bars" and "hooks"). And even the vowels could connect the students to their old lives of fear (the *e*'s look like "spying eyes" or "fists"); but this more primeval sound, as it is represented, begins to look like a seed. The meaningless *tree*, made up of such seeds, may cause "forests and gardens" to "spring in their heads." The seed of hope, of life, is in the symbolic word.

What new place with what new language awaits her dead father in "Voyager"? And what "bundle of time"? In a vision from memory recorded in "Bread and Apples," the "pages of the history book / he leafs through keep springing back to the beginning." In "Midnight" her long-dead grandfather waves to her from a "photograph in her head," calling her home across the sea, calling her back to an earlier time as if it were indeed possible for her to return. She looks at the negative of a photo of her father in "Voyager": the inversion of light and dark represents the inversion in time and perhaps a re-version of reality.

Lisel Mueller's fascination with the elasticity of time was apparent in "Pallindrome" (*Life of a Queen*, 1970), written from a suggestion in *Scientific American* that "Intelligent beings in each galaxy" might "regard their own time as 'forward' and time in the other galaxy as 'backward.'" She writes, "Somewhere, sometime," she and her alter ego "must have / passed one another like going and coming trains, / with both of us looking the other way." Time passing, as in a newsreel, a film which can go backwards or forwards, is illustrated in "Beginning in 1914" (*The Need to Hold Still*, 1980), which records the history, as she remembers it, of her family. The film of her memory can be speeded up through the earlier parts or, as in "time-lapse photography," display the "inchmeal growth of daughters," until film becomes the present and "I am playing myself." But her "playing" now will become film in the future.

Lisel Mueller said of her poems in *The Need to Hold Still* (1980), "I'm trying to make connections, looking for links between where we have been and where we are going." The connections between the past and the present are well perceived, as she discovered while studying folklore, in fairy tales and legends. Because these stories are told in metaphor, the critical experiences of our ancestors, generation after generation, become accessible to us and applicable to our own lives. In the preface to *The Need to Hold Still*, she quoted William Stafford:

> So the world happens twice—
> Once what we see it as;
> Second, it legends itself
> deep, the way it is.

Fairy tales and legends inhabit much of Lisel Mueller's poetry. The long poem "Voices from the Forest" (the title poem in the volume, 1977), is a history of humankind told by many of the archetypes of legend, a history that repeats itself in every generation: "Your story does not end / with the wedding dance, it goes on." Folk tales tell us what makes us human. In "Why We Tell Stories" (*The Need to Hold Still*, 1980), she answers the question: "because we awakened / and learned to speak." Folk tales show us the universality and continuity of life: "each of us tells / the same story / but tells it differently . . . ." Each new generation says, "we will begin our story / with the word *and*." In "The Story," from the same volume, a parent reads to the children a tale that disturbs him: "Make up your own / ending, you say to the children, / and they will, they will."

Such stories, like poetry, look at the heart, at the riddle, and accept the mystery, as do children, the innocent heroes of so many fairy tales, whose wings are not fully clipped (This Sadness, This Happiness, *The Need to Hold Still*, 1980), whose drawings are always of smiling families outside the house, the chimney of which, though it is summer, cosily smokes (Drawings by Children, *The Need to Hold Still*, 1980). Children and tellers of stories (and poets) see and accept the incongruous. So, in "Bread and Apples," the child "does not ask who made bread / in an uninhabited wilderness," and the poet accepts her dead father's unbidden presence, just as she accepts in "Voyager" that her father could have safely arrived in a new place, and might believe in

"Midnight" that the sea, which separates her from her dead grandfather "standing on a boardwalk" in a photograph in her head, "would part for my long walk home."

"After Whistler" is one of Lisel Mueller's several poems inspired by a painting, in this instance "The Little White Girl." The whiteness of the girl's dress and the fragility of her face and body remind the poet of the fairy tales in which swan-girls cannot fit into their sharply defined environment and sub-consciously remember another home, a snow world. Mueller describes such a place in "First Snow in Lake County" (*Dependencies*, 1965):

> a place, a time
> untouched and uncorrupted
> The world before we were here.

Nor can these girls be happy in the bright sun, with the regulation and conformity, the glittering reality around them. The misfit chooses the moon to be the guide, chooses the mystery, the "precious aberra-tion," rather than full light and rationality. The moon has long represented inconsistency, inaccessibility, and mystery. "Moonfishing" (*Dependencies*, 1965) tells of the compulsion to catch the moon with sharp and round utensils, with women's hair, with hearts and lips and tongues, but of the inevitable and nec-essary failure. The wise fisherman in "Mermaid," from the same volume, knows that to possess mys-tery is to destroy it and that we cannot live without mystery.

In "A Farewell, A Welcome" (*The Private Life*, 1976), written after the lunar landings, Mueller says goodbye to the moon as mystery, but not to mys-tery itself: "women will spill their blood / in spite of you now   lunatics wave goodbye / accepting despair by another name." Because we have "in-vaded the moon," she says in "The End of Science Fiction" (*The Need to Hold Still*, 1980), because "We are the gods who can unmake / the world in seven days," we need to recreate the old myths to save us, we need to find our mystery again, to

> Invent a man and a woman
> naked in a garden,
> invent a child that will save the world
> . . . .
> a girl who grows into a tree

a woman who refuses to turn
her back on the past and is changed into salt.

Technology wishes to keep us, as it were, in the full light of the sun and restrict our sight to what we can really see. But Mary Shelley in "The Triumph of Life" admonishes the twentieth century reader/writer, "You don't trust the heart . . . the center, the real thing," and she reminds us that it is the spirit that will win in the end, the word that will survive the body.

Despite technology, survival itself remains a mys-tery. The "Why me?" that the survivor (as well as the victim) may well ask is a perpetual question that is never really answered and one that has filled Mueller with wonder, even awe, and perhaps with a tinge of guilt. In "Twelve Hours in March" (*Life of a Queen*, 1970), the narrator awakens and

> The morning news locates the dead
> in another country;
> The surgeon's knife sharpens for someone else.
> Our children did not drown in the well; listen,
> Their voices balloon in the house.
> *Spared, Spared* they shout
> In the careless language of gods.

Mueller is aware that, while she is spared, someone else suffers. While she walks safely and happily on a Sunday morning with her husband, suddenly there flashes in her mind a picture of a tortured Algerian girl, ". . . my antilife, / with her dark red wound." (Untitled, *The Private Life*, 1976) While many others suffered the effects of the war, she was spared death and despair in Germany: "America saved me. . . . I was not crushed under rubble, nor was I beaten / along a frozen highway; my children are not dead / of post-war hunger." (On Reading an Anthology of Postwar German Poetry, *The Private Life*, 1976)

Beyond the gift of survival is the gift of good for-tune: some people acquire the "survivor's art," like her parents, who could "pull joy from any borrowed hat." (Voyager) Good fortune, like survival, is a mys-tery which one merely accepts. In "The Third Son's Confession" from "Voices from the Forest" (1977), the legendary lucky hero cannot explain:

> Don't ask me if I was chosen
> or simply lucky. Years ago

I threw a penny down a well
and made a wish, that's all.

In "For Lucy" (*Dependencies*, 1965) Mueller says, "Magic? Who knows, who knows / what rites persuade our luck . . . ." And in "A Real Toad in a Real Garden" (The Private Life, 1976), she says, "Blessings / come in strange shapes and sizes / . . . who knows / . . . what / supernatural sponsor / of healthy children and natural death . . . ?"

"Chances Are" looks not only at the unpredictability and inexplicability of survival, but also at the irony and paradox in life that show up in a single newspaper page: while one hundred children are ruthlessly slaughtered in one part of the world, a woman without a uterus miraculously gives birth in another. Death and birth are conjunct: Mary Shelley reminds us, "my mother died / of my birth." And "Report to the National Commission on Violence" (*The Private Life*, 1976) points out that being conceived and born, then loving, conceiving, and giving birth oneself, all incorporate competititon to survive. "Chances Are" tells us what we'd prefer to forget: that, whereas every seed represents hope, few seeds grow to fruition. For human beings, it is the poor who most clearly represent that Darwinian principle: they "bank on the waste of numbers / to insure the single life." (Monarchs, *The Private Life*, 1976) The woman in Ohio, full of hope for her child, sensually aware of its tugging needs for nutrition, does not want to believe in bleak ratios for survival, and dreams, instead, of a land without competition and violence, without the need to hope for miracles. Such fantasies are necessary "to make just dreams / out of our unjust lives." (Reading the Brothers Grimm to Jenny, *The Private Life*, 1976)

In another irony, the victim that does not want to die has its counterpart in the survivor that does not wish to survive. Mary Shelley says that, after her children died:

> For months I wanted to be
> with those three small bodies
> to be still in a dark place

In "Widow" the survivor wants to eat "the food of the dead," the "dry, black seeds" of hope for death. She wants to unglue her soul so that it might emigrate to the country where her husband is; she wants to break the code of the dead and learn their language.

Or one can overrule chance and refuse the luck of the survivor, like the suicide in "About Suffering They Were Never Wrong." Mueller takes her title from W. H. Auden's "Musée des Beaux Arts," which observes that the "old masters" knew and exposed in their paintings the true nature of suffering—that it takes place alone and unobserved. In her poem, however, and in earlier ones, she points out what artists *don't* tell. In "Testimony" (*The Need to Hold Still*, 1980) Venus tells how Botticelli painted her, coming to birth and shore with "rose-tipped breasts / lifting toward the sun," and how he imagined that she stepped into "shoes of glittering white sand." But she remembers that "the rocks and shells cut into my feet." She felt "cold and lost." The artist sees what he wants to see, not what the model feels. The model in "The Artist's Model, ca. 1912" (*The Need to Hold Still*, 1980) speaks for all women who have been painted by men, recounting that modern artists have distorted women's bodies through impressionism, cubism, neo-primitivism, and any other "ism" which labels their visions. The artists tell the model that, in the future, women will be represented only by their parts: "a gigantic pair of lips, / a nipple, slick as candy." Finally, even the parts will disappear. The model then responds, "you will look for me / in the air . . . / . . . inside your head, / where I started, your own work of art." Painters reproduce only what they wish to see.

If painters do not get beneath surfaces to represent the actual person, neither, Mueller confesses in "In Praise of Surfaces" (*Life of a Queen*, 1970), can she know the full mystery of one with whom she has been intimate for a long time. She says to her husband, "*one flesh* is all / the mystery we were promised." And she admits, "Words, too, are surfaces / scraped or shaken loose. . . ."

So the neighbors, like painters, like most observers, in "About Suffering" have focused on the body and the house, which tell nothing of the essence of the woman who killed herself or why she did so. Her windows, like her body, were opaque, her speech only a diversion: the surfaces were merely misleading. The woman inside both house and body concealed, as a computer stores "chips," her memories and secrets, the most significant of which silently, and on a day which confused autumn with spring, death with birth, became too big to remain intact. This pregnancy, however, "imploded," and what it gave birth to disappeared when she did.

If one continues to survive, one, of course, ages. The person within the body watches the mirror with incredulity as the face and body become strangers. In "Fugitive" the aging woman feels her true self to be in disguise, a humorous, incongruous disguise to which she unprotestingly submits. Nobody can see who she really is, the same essence that she has always been, an essence, moreover, that has grown more valuable as it has gotten more compact—all the memories, all the experiences of the girl, the young woman, and the mature woman in one. In "A Nude by Edward Hopper" (*Life of a Queen*, 1970), another aging woman speaks from within her body, which has been displayed by the artist as "used," "scant," "a patch of lavender cells." The portrayal is not as she might see herself or might wish to be seen: "A man's dream / of heat and softness." Her body hides much more than it shows: "my childhood / is buried here . . . desire / crested and wore itself thin / between these bones . . . ." "This body / is home," she says. But whereas this woman's cry is plaintive in the desire to be truly seen and known, the speaker in "Fugitive" wishes to elude the pursuers of her secret self: "No one suspects / its value." Who can see the electricity in the unassuming "power line"? Gleefully, she runs away with life, savoring the hoax, fully aware of the treasure she carries within her. "Fugitive" is one of Mueller's lightly humorous poems. (The Egg, *The Need to Hold Still*, 1980, is another.)

Wry, rather than light, though on the same topic of the aging woman, is "After the Facelift." This face, too, belies the woman within, but she is attempting to go backward in time as though she has never been there. She has "removed . . . years," has "yanked" them off "in the wrong direction." The imprints from pain, from all feelings, from experiences, are gone. There is no history in her face; it "reveals nothing." She has wished to eradicate time. The narrator, equally old but with a naturally old face, watches bemused as the forty-year-old woman with the thirty-year-old face surrounds herself with greens, among them curly endive, smooth feminine shaped peppers—symbols of youth and voluptuous-

ness. Finally, as she "moves ahead," she reaches for the first flowers of the season, as though she can actually try youth again.

Perhaps she has "betrayed" her husband by yanking off the years together with him. Not so the speaker in "Up North," who cannot see the age in her husband because her "eyes have changed at the same rate." Though there are faint warnings of winter's coming—a few birds "flying back," a few red leaves—the two of them dawdle, like red tomatoes, as they did the summer before, unaware, unafraid of what is coming. Nor has either selfishly kept anything from the other (as the plums do) to prepare for what is coming. Growing old seems easy when it is shared in love. In Mueller's first poem in her first book, "The Blind Leading the Blind," *Dependencies* (1965), there is that same sense of comfort and awe with a lover, but at a younger age, when it is darker, and movement and preparation must be made: "There are two of us in this cave / . . . . Touch me." The need for love, for family, has been made clear throughout Lisel Mueller's poetry: her husband, her parents and grandparents, and her daughters have given her a sense of meaning and continuity (see, for instance, "My Grandmother's Gold Pin," *Life of a Queen*, 1970).

Lisel Mueller says in the preface to her translation of the German poet Marie Luise Kaschnitz (1980): "Above all she is a poet of continuities, the continuity of nature and the continuity of history, that is, human consciousness." The same could be said for Mueller herself. In the later poems, as well as throughout her earlier poems, she has shown connections: between human beings and the rest of nature (Life of a Queen, 1970); between people of all times and places (Voices from the Forest, 1977); between the living and the dead (Signs, *The Need to Hold Still*, 1980). She emphasizes our debt to our predecessors (Historical Museum, *The Private Life*, 1976). And particularly she shows how life is perpetually renewed through the cycles of birth, love, death, and birth again (Thriving Season, *Dependencies*, 1965).

She also said of Kaschnitz, "The loss of demarcations between places and periods of time, which occurs in old age, served her well as a metaphor." As Lisel Mueller herself looks toward old age, it is fitting that the collection of her poems in this anthology, as well as this essay, ends with "Monet Refuses the Operation." Monet does not want modern technology to repair his sight (as Mary Shelley would not have wanted "capsules and doctors / . . . kits for paper flowers" to cure her grief; she knew, wisely, that feelings must be felt). His cataracts enable him to see inwardly and to see beneath surfaces. It has taken him a lifetime to repair his own erroneous youthful sight. Only now can he see the continuities in the universe, that the "world / is flux." (Mueller had seen in "Merce Cunningham and the Birds," *The Need to Hold Still*, 1980, that "the world / is energy.") Only now can Monet see that everything and everyone are part of each other, that they are continually striving to re-embrace their separateness, and that there is no end to time and space. Surely,

Lisel Mueller, too, has been working toward a similar vision: of a universe without boundaries and a journey without end.

Editor's Note: Poems that appear in Lisel Mueller's published books are noted by source where discussed in the Critical Response. Those that have no source noted are from her new manuscript *Second Language*; many of these quoted poems appear in this anthology. A list of Mueller's published books appears in our biography of her.

ROBERTA SIMONE received her Ph.D. in English at the University of Illinois in 1965. She teaches at Grand Valley State College in Allendale, Michigan, where she is Associate Professor of English and Chair-elect of the department. She lives in Grand Haven, Michigan, a lovely, lakeside town. She has two grown children and has published verse in *Light Year*, '85.

Ardyth Bradley

LIBERTYVILLE, ILLINOIS

Hospital

Everything stops, he said.
No. It goes on snowing.

    What vows could I make?—
    that I would welcome the snow,
    touch everything with skinned fingers?
    I would sink back,
    I would mourn the passage of time,
    I would fear future troubles,
    I would continue my life.

Tape it on, I asked; though
I'd had it off many times—had even
bought it myself for $17,
since my groom had had no money.
But the finger would swell.
So off came 20 years—or whatever
status as a protected species
the ring had conferred for 20 years.
Perhaps breasts too are merely institutions,
and life is a plain, stitched heart
pounding
ringless.

    In the operating room something kept
      beeping.
    My heartbeat!
    Everyone could hear how fast
    it went, with, occasionally,
    three quick stutters.

In bed I could touch a button to switch TV
    channels.
At some unpredicted point as I flashed from show to
    show
the TV would always turn off and the screen go
    suddenly blank.

    Once as I stood in the hall
    the doors of the down elevator slid open.
      Empty,
    it waited a moment before closing again,
    but I would not go in.

With whom does that crow
riding the branch
communicate?
The trees?
And wind?

Every part lonely.

The wind is saying. . . .

I can say
I have you

    I must live now like a saint: despite everything.
    Or like a mouse tunneling under the snow,
    direction unknown in the dim white,
    remembering only to dig and gnaw.

Phebe Hanson

ST. PAUL, MINNESOTA

First Friend

Make a list of all the friends you ever had, beginning with Delores Morrison, the newspaper editor's daughter who lived across the alley in your hometown of Sacred Heart, Minnesota, the two of you in your flowered beach pajamas, California dream brought to those dry backyards, Hollywood blossoming on little girls who made mudpies from pump water and caked dirt which wouldn't grow gardens, both of you squinting into the sun for the picture her mother was taking, her thin brown arm around your plump one, your squat firm body against her tall slender one, you in sunbleached bangs, she in dark curls, she more languid and exotic, seeming worldly even at eight, up in her bedroom which she shared with no one, an only child, you never having known the terror of privacy, the bliss of having your own room, envying her movie star splendor, you lying on her white chenille bedspread playing doctor, taking turns lying there in your cotton bloomers and thin-strapped summer undershirts, you feeling her cool hands pulling down your bloomers, separating the lips of your vagina, looking seriously at them as only a doctor would, Dr. Dordahl who never that you could remember had looked down there, all he had ever done was take your adenoids out as you lay under the ether swirls in his office, spinning into infinite colored concentric circles, waking to the smell which tainted your nostrils even when you bent over the roses in your back yard, hoping their smell would replace it, now she was looking there, into that blossom at the bottom of your stomach, she was looking where even your doctor had never looked, and she was pretending to be the doctor and you accepted the solemn look on her face, you believed what she saw was serious and important even while you felt the strangeness of her fingers there, where not even your own fingers nor the fingers of your doctor had been, she was your first friend, you did what she wanted you to do because she was older, and when she thought it would be a good idea for the two of you to squat over the opening, the little grate in the floor of her bed room and piss there, you did that too, because it was part of the solemnity and excitement of playing doctor, and it was only the next day when her mother took you both into the dining room and showed you the ugly spreading yellow stain in the ceiling wallpaper that you knew you couldn't be friends any more. Later she moved away and you never saw her again.

Nursing

Now I mostly remember
   how hard they pulled,
the unbelievable strength
   in those small mouths,
the smell of faintly sour milk
   drying on my dress,
the sunlight that fell
   across the bed
early mornings when I took
   them out of their cribs

to hold them between my breast
    and their father's back.
How I worried they would
    never get enough
because my mother-in-law
    kept telling me
to give them formula so what
    they got was regulated.
Now I remember that's all
    there was for me to do then:

eat right so they would
    be well-nourished,
drink plenty of liquids
    so the milk would flow.
I remember thinking
    even God
wouldn't strike me down
    while I was nursing.
It's the only time
    I felt really safe.

Meat

I dream I go out to dinner
with a visiting poet,
his hair curling black into his beard.
I am pleased that he seems to like me,
seems to want to go out to dinner with me.

We stand at a long counter
ordering beef to go for the children.
Thick rare slabs.
The order comes to $4.58.
I write the check.
They dish up the meat in countless black cast-iron pans,
rows and rows of them,
more meat than we can carry between us,
so much meat,
too much meat for the children.

We begin to load the meat in the black iron pans
onto carts and then onto elevators,
for now we seem to be in the lobby
of a dingy and mysterious hotel.
The poet is on the elevator
which has stopped a few feet below floor level
and I am handing him down the endless pans of meat.
It takes forever.
I know we will never get to dinner.
I think of Sisyphus.
We are like Sisyphus!
I am pleased at last to be dreaming an archetypal dream!
The poet is in the corner of the elevator,
and as I reach down to hand him yet another pan
I accidentally unhook a latch.
The elevator drops almost an entire floor,
and the poet lurches, loses his balance.

I can still see him, below me, surrounded by the pans of meat.
Furious, he is furious at me.

Now I am in the bedroom of an old farmhouse
in the midst of a snowstorm.
The poet has a new plan for getting the meat into the house.
He has hooked the pans together,
an endless chain of cast-iron pans,
each with its steaming chunk of rare roast beef,
and he is climbing up the long sloping roof
toward my bedroom window,
pulling the pans with one hand,
dragging himself slowly up the roof with the other.
I lean out the window to offer my hands in help;
he grasps my hands with both of his,
forgets and lets go of the pans.
They slide off the roof with a frightful clatter.
He looks back, loses his balance.
I can still see him, below me, surrounded by the pans of meat.
Furious, he is furious at me.

I go down into the snow farmyard below
where many children, many people are doing farm chores.
I am in a Breughel painting!
I am pleased to be dreaming of Breughel!
I look for my poet.
He is going through piles of manure and snow and straw,
looking for the meat.
He will not look at me.
I feel great sadness.
I know the meat by now is ruined,
that we will never go out for dinner,
that the children will never eat.

I leave the farmyard, go into the house.
It is elegant, heavy with antique furniture,
Russian in feeling.
I am in a Tolstoy novel!
This is truly a high-class dream!
I pass through the dining room into a small dark room
at the back of the house.
It is a room in our old house in Sacred Heart.
Back in a corner, a woman lies on a daybed, napping.
I walk over to her, kneel beside her, tell her of my sadness.
She wakes, turns to me; it is my mother.
She offers me a pan of meat
from the table beside the daybed.

Kathleen Norris

LEMMON, SOUTH DAKOTA

The First Day of Summer

Shadehill, South Dakota, 1975

This is earth.
Cedars, a cottonwood
Frame the kitchen door.
Two horses are grazing
Near the old house,
Where lovers awaken, year after year.

They are still living,
Some of them.
The Indian camp is only rocks
And a view, the wagon trail
Just a deeper green through the draw.
Fields planted a month ago
Are a far country.

Here they ate, brushing off flies:
They talked, drinking whiskey,
And the beds sang all night
Above the kitchen where a woman sits
Listening, still,
As long trees close the door.

Visitors

Shadehill, South Dakota, 1975

The view from the guest room:
Sheep grazing to the north,
Two horses running.
Children play at a well
Where a stand of trees is now.

We are watching
Through windows of old glass:
A wintry smear
On the boy, who moves like a god,
Giving names to things. Here,
A white-bell, and the homesteader's lean-to.
Over there,
Aiglagya, where Indians hunted.
What were they like?
The earth lies open,
Well-worked.
Father and son
Speak to each other in hard phrases.
They are walking through the grass.

On the Northwest Hiawatha

Up the coast from Seattle, then east into the mountains. A full moon.

Where there are mountains, there are rivers. Our sleeping car is called: "Skykomish River."

Sleep torn apart, in the upper bunk. Forbidden territory. I remember that, and the Pullman being taken down; the funny fold-up toilet; and in the dining car, yellow flowers in a glass vase. A crisp tablecloth. There are children on this train, to remember other things. The people I traveled to see then are dead.

Near dawn. A man outside Paradise, Montana, carries a long metal rod through a field. He balances like a trapeze artist.

My husband is still sleeping. I go alone to the dining car. We stop in Missoula, where two men are asleep in the yard, lying against a building, in the shade. The building looks old.

I read, without much interest, in the dome car. As we cross the Continental Divide, a man across the aisle says:
    "Of course, I've seen this before."
    "Three times," the man's wife adds.
"You know a fact when you see one, Archie," Nero Wolfe is saying, "but you have no feeling for phenomena."

My husband is half-dressed, looking out the window. "Are we still in Montana?" he asks.

We speed by the edges of towns, large frame houses sliced by afternoon shadow. Something is going on inside all the houses: conversations, mysteries.

Night again, and I look for names of towns in the neon glare: John Deere, American Legion Post, A and W Root Beer. I imagine lovers walking under trees. Streetlights give the trees a stage-show gaudiness that the lovers do not notice. I imagine a doctor and an undertaker, deep in talk, leaning on a bar.

Fires along a river. A string of fires. People move in and out of the small red halos.

Even in the dark, one learns the land: farms far apart, the human fabric worn thin. We move closer to my grandmother's garden, rich with earthworms and manure: to the bed where my mother was born: where we will sleep, again, tomorrow.

Cary Waterman

MANKATO, MINNESOTA

A Light in the Doorway

"Anything approaching us we try to understand, say,
Like a lamp being carried up a lane at midnight."
                    Norman Dubie, *In the Dead of the Night*

It is late afternoon
just beginning to lose light.
This is the graveyard of the day
when you think you will not move again
either forward or backward.
And it is raining, slowly.
The reflections on the road
are like images on a seal's back
washing through a black wave.

Still my father-in-law drives,
nervously, carefully,
as he has all his life.
And he has little to say
as the car tires disappear into
these reflections
as into a drama,
then reappear on the other side
like an audience clapping.

Along the way a door is opened to a house
through which pale light comes
like that which comes from the underwings of moths.
A man has just entered the house,
has just come home from killing something.
He carries a black lunchbox
into which he has put the final tones
of the afternoon.

He loves his children who leap toward him
through this shaft of light.
He loves his wife standing with white dishes
like wafers of love in her hands.
His shoulders are damp with rain.
And with sea water.
In this ceremony he has left the door open
so that the other lives that pursue him
may come or go as they wish.

Linda M. Hasselstrom

HERMOSA, SOUTH DAKOTA

Leaving Fargo: April

The highway's lined with dead black drifts.
Wind tries to push me back north.
Trucks lean like whales into the storm.
Gray trees crawl the horizon;
plowed fields mist, dissolve behind me.
A lean black dog, missing since
December, has emerged from
a roadside ditch to die again
in an April blizzard, winter
resurrected.

The Poet Falls in Love
with a Cowboy

I'm going home like a section line road,
straight and fast, past empty houses
crouched on hills, past a cat
sniffing the snow wind, coyote tracks
scribbled on a drift, smooth

heifers with blank white faces,
Hereford bulls with icy horns.
Horses, heads bowed, are backed
into the storm. It mounts, plunges
on. The wheels pull the road under me.

A section line road never makes a smooth
womanly curve; it hangs a hard left,
and this wasn't supposed to be your poem.
But you're a man of that land and I can't
keep you out. You're a walking chunk
of the Grand River breaks: bobcats stalk
your skull, grouse nest in your hollows,
coyotes prowl ridges of sinew. If I were
your woman, I'd be rolling north, not south,
finding a straight road to a hidden cow camp.

If I ever see you again, it will be
from the armchair by my own fire, or some
motel room, some airport, some other road
I'll drive, reminding winter that it
owes me mercy.

When My Father Waters His Trees

                    he puts the hose
in the fifty-gallon drum, stands in the shade till
it's full. Doorless, the green '49 Chevy truck
grates, starts, lumbers out of the yard. The running boards,
still black, snap; the jack rattles; the windshield wiper
on the floor bounces left and right. One fender is
beginning to sag but the boards in the box are
new oak. The glove box is wired shut and contains one

pair of wire clippers and a cigarette pack
put there in 1956 when Dad stopped smoking.

                My father says
the green truck starts when it's too cold
for the new one. He pulls up to the tree row, dips
a bucket out, pours it on the first tree, slowly
walks back for another, arms swinging. It's evening,
he's been haying all day; he fills and then empties
the drum several times, waits for a late supper.

                Sometimes
I hear the old truck start just before dawn,
while it's cool. On last year's birthday I heard him say,
"Well, I'm 69. Shall I quit, or should I plant
more trees?"

                He got twenty cedar from the Forest Service,
took his long-handled spade out northeast of the house.
Most of the shoots are a foot high now, growing green.

Shooting Prairie Dogs

I lie down in the short grass,
sight on a fat brown pup. His
shrill voice pipes over dirt mounds.
He bobs down, up, tail twitching.

                Shot at,
he doesn't run but
sits up, paws folded against
his chest, looks for the overhead whine.

                Hit, he
jerks, topples, drops. When I kick him,
he rolls over, bloody, moving with fleas
like a migrating blanket.

                Holes he's dug
stand for years, traps for horses
to snap legs in, dens for snakes. Grass
killed by his digging takes years to return,
damage hard to calculate in dollars.

Here I am, who marched behind Martin Luther King,
who stood the taunts behind a sign that read "Silent
Vigil against the War," ran like everyone else
when the flying wedge of cops hit the quadrangle,
here I am, shooting prairie dogs, thinking like J.
Edgar Hoover after Kent State.

                I shoot again.
The dog falls in his hole; his heart lies on the edge,
quivering.

Patricia Hooper

BIRMINGHAM, MICHIGAN

Deer in the Open Field

1

They are there from the beginning.
Sometimes they move toward you
shyly, until you notice.
Long ago, as a child, you saw them
and followed their tracks for hours
through deep grass. Finally
you knew you had lost them and stood
farther off than you intended,
grass stretching in every direction
and none of it bent or parted
to show where the deer had vanished.
It was late evening, and far
in the distance you saw your house
the size of a stone, and your brothers
had entered and shut the door
on the field forever.

2

Many things choose you: grass
harnessed in sunlight, leaves
stammering, stones
hushed in a courtyard.

And always the wildflowers—
their bodies blowing like seas,
simple as water.

You know them.
But the others who come toward you
with their field-breath, their furred antlers,
you love more.

When they nuzzle your hand,
they are saying *Name me*, their bodies
pleading, their eyes like your eyes,
lucid and vulnerable.

3

Their season. Again the crimson
maples, the hills ignited,
the seeds frantic.

And milkweed—
where shall it set down
its mild cargo?

As if, on a battlefield,
a creature should give birth,

so the pods open,
releasing
a weightlessness unasked for,
like the soul's,

till, in the mud,
the seeds, barely visible,
writhe from their tents of feathers.

And overhead
gunshot,
the startled animals,

a field of husks.

4

You wait for a long time
in your life, which you were given.

Finally a door opens:
you step forth from the house
and there is the sun, already
sweeping the field, and trees
whose names you had not forgotten,
fastened in frost like armor,
so dazzling, so inventive
you know you will walk toward them
in spite of the wildflowers
asleep in their glass prisms
and the sky, bone-white, unentreating.
You see them, not far off,
gathered, their antlers lifted
from the deep grasses, in welcome,
while back of you, as before,
the dust wakes on the doorsill
and light touches the wall
as it did so many times
when you were living.

The Window

The field drifts into darkness.
From my window I make out
the edge of the porch, no further.
Finally the stars regather;
unmended, the moon moves forth.

Night after night, I've seen it.
Drying the dishes, or scouring,
I've looked up, in my kitchen,
and noticed the sun dissolving,
flame after flame, into cloud.

Into deep, fathomless blackness.
They say that the stars are leaving
vast holes when they perish. I need
no evidence but believe this
earnestly. As I study

black glass for a trace of road,
it is as if the table
and the voices from bedrooms, even
the walls of the kitchen, were severed
behind me, from where I stand

staring out into infinite absence.
And I think, *Let something be out there,*
a fox or a deer. . . . In daylight
deer stood in the field. Now I see them
in memory, standing attentive

at the row of birches beyond
the path to the barn. They will not
come closer, although I would ask it
if I knew how. If I knew
the way, I would summon a road

and a lamp further off, a window
where someone stands squinting at something
believable in the distance.
Then I could believe the barn
and the deer at the edge of it, even

my breath on the glass as I move
past the moon into emptiness, stars
going dark in the universe . . . drifting
like an astronaut, clutching these lifelines:
this towel, this plate in my hand.

Mary Trimble

CHICAGO, ILLINOIS

Now and Again

    Dazed lightning,
white moths flush from the curtains.
    From your chair
you nod at the lit field,
    book open,
hands smoothing the pages.
    You recall
a bulldog named Spike,
    a small boy
who might have been you,
    running home
in front of the summer storm.
    Heart pounding,
he stood at the kitchen window
    watching rain clouds
black out the skyline around the farm.
    In lamplight,
the empty house quiet as held breath,
    he stands watching
white moths beat on the window pane.

Dislocation

Somewhere west of here,
framed by a black prairie,
you are walking the line of the day.

The old feelings,
obstinate as history,
leading you into ambush.

You are thinking
of staying home from school, a boy,
touching forbidden porcelain

on the mantelpiece.
Your mother's voice
weeps over the pieces.

No one is ever forgiven.
Sad rowhouses disappear
into the city of past tenses

and you are walking through fields
of medieval wheat
pressed over the earth like gold leaf,

the million heads bowing yes, yes

Port Letter

When we sailed
    into the white cities of Phoenicia,
you were my son;

my hand
    fit both of yours inside,
small as walnuts.

You played all day
    on the deck with my necklace
of blue stones

and the sailors said,
    "It is lucky, blue eyes, the sea
knows you are

one of us."
    Little squirrel, men spoke of destiny
as you tossed and caught

blue stones,
    stuffing them into your cheeks.
All that day

my heart was beating
    for a face deep in the white city.
Now I remember

rocking you in the heat.
    We were a small breath, clouding
the glass of the water.

Margo LaGattuta

ROCHESTER, MICHIGAN

Asking the Windows

I am crawling out
of the sound
of my own voice
forgetting things
I am learning
what I've always known
I take pictures
develop them in glue
put my finger
through a hole
in the window
the air
erases me
my house
doesn't know I exist
the walk
to the front door
gets longer
I have taken to sleeping
on your side of the bed
when I wake up
I'm not there
and you
can't forget me

Margot Kriel

ST. PAUL, MINNESOTA

Chokecherry Summers

What I didn't know in that photograph
of North Dakota summer, I see thirty
years later: my mother's skirt fanned
a flame from the bucket of bitter fruit.
Growing each year in its heat,
I would forget everything
but my sister's mouth,
red with plum juice.

Recreate the summer I slept
on pantry shelves, under paraffin,
like our field rabbit
who escaped in the lettuce I saw
grandfather cover with sugar and cream.
Rabbit in flowered bowl
cut awake by knife and fork.
I howled red grief
in his folded napkin,
trembling, caught in its silver ring.

Next summer, imprisoned
in backstairs tower,
I heard them, mother
and grandfather, plot
in the kitchen
to bury me
in bureau drawers.
There I discovered
they'd murdered her, too,
grandmother, lavender,
our faces mirrored
like legs
from her one bobby pin.

My mother the daughter,

lighting the stove,
making the beds. The summer
I ran three miles to Lake Elsie,
calling for father, always the absent.
The hot August morning
blood ran down my legs,
I hated my mother
in her separate white room.
She cut me a patch
from grandfather's shirt.
She didn't tell me,
each day I wore him,
slowly he'd die.

Finally a summer with Father
away from Dakota, his big toe
soaked epsom salts. I baited
hooks bread for him, cut
index-card houses, bed, table,
and chairs, wanted
to marry him,
but he only played violin
with me at piano,
home from the train.

Now I walk to the lake
with chokecherry, plum,
and speak to a farmer
scything a meadow.
I want to crown the years
with thistle's pink head.
But my sister's turned singer,
red mapled hill,
and grandfather lives with a stone.
Only his shirt sleeve,
matted with dirt,
waits by the road.

Janet Beeler Shaw

MADISON, WISCONSIN

Photo by Mark Beeler

The Divorce Poem

The whole village was burning,
the grass along the river a snake of fire.
Behind us my pots lay broken,
our bed overthrown,
the family graves torn open.
I pulled my daughter by her small hand,
running, crying out my son!
for he fell behind
and I have not found him.

The boat was old and crowded.
As we drew away from shore,
I saw the bonfires shrink to candles
guttering out in the waves.
My broken ribs tore my breath
as I asked each one around me,
Have you seen a boy with yellow hair?
Perhaps I was searching for you as well.

For a little while grey water curled
at my feet like our cat, and the last light
tasted of the sweat of sleeping children.
Then the wind pressed its face against mine,
its mouth sharp as a knife blade,
and we rowed into an open sea
that does not end.

The Handless Maiden

Once there was a miller who wished to marry
his daughter to the Devil in exchange for
gold. When she refused, her father cut off
her hands . . .

Suddenly the house had no doors.
I cried Daddy! Daddy! to stop him
but the pain came down
and my hands fell onto the floor
in front of me like kittens,
fingers curled around my thumbs,
hiding my thumbs.
I wanted to pick up my hands
in my teeth and carry them away
to a nest, but there wasn't time.

I ran and then I crawled,
turning back to lick up the blood trace
so he couldn't find my trail.
The forest closed behind me,
branches locked like arms guarding,
an insignia of sun on the pines.

That night I lay next to a fallen log
as though it were my mother.
My dream tasted of metal.
When I woke in the wet leaves
I knew it was not a dream.

All winter I listened to the snow
Whisper of what must not be given away.
No! grew as round in my mouth as an apple.
My teeth broke the green skin
and I tasted the tart lesson:
I had held out my hands
when my father commanded me
Although I saw his knife.

When the white trees blossomed like milk,
I felt the itch of new fingers
Unfurling, crisp as crocuses,
from the buds of my wounds.

Maureen Bloomfield

CINCINNATI, OHIO

Photo by Valerie Shesko

Clara Schumann at the Piano

As if you'd sketched a fern
Then dragged an eraser along the edge
Not from misjudgment—
Elms grow out of water, clouds of glass
Until the viola echoes
And I walk out of myself, this room's
Limestone columns, leaded windows
Even as I nod to Catherine to turn the page.

We walked in the garden in August
Deep baskets on our arms.
For the roses, I loved best
The ones like nacre,
Almost blue, as if not quite alive
And cold, against my glove.
I enter with the cello, remembering
The day we chose our life
With such tight-lipped resolution.

But you have never asked
More than I can give and freely.
You, I—the indistinction
Repeats, is answered.
I look up, I find
Your eyes. The *agitato* cracks the glass
Elms in the gray water, black keys—
I feel the world break up and build
Again, imperfect but our own.

Karin Kania

OAK PARK, MICHIGAN

Revisiting Detroit

(after Robert Dana's reading)

I am staring at the moon
and reflecting on the circle
a child's mouth makes
when in pain. I am
remembering a circle
a stranger implanted
in my head like cobalt
or hot lead. I am
remembering a man
so heavy and a burning
so deep I still scream
to it at night. And a rocking,
a rocking that couldn't get out.
God, is there no end to it,
no distance, no one place
where one can swerve
left or right and find herself
on I-96 heading toward Flint,
where nothing original happens,
or 66 into the dry Midwest?
On a night this thick,
with the air so rich
I could drink it or eat it
from a spoon, I focus
on my own imminent death,
which the doctors term
pre-malignant. I concentrate
on something black running
into a hole under the steps
of the Belcrest Hotel,
to surface between the floorboards
in another child's world.

I hold that child's tears
in the corner of my eyes
like stones, and tell no one
of the seeds she grinds
between her teeth after sundown,
or of the solemn duty she pulls
stuffing glass into ratholes.
I am on the terrace of the Belcrest,
pretending I like beer
and celebrating the clapping
of hands for a poet's
last reading. I am trapped
in the essence of creating
small noises in academic circles,
clinking glasses together
and swallowing the month of May
like rainwater,
and recalling when hell was
this visible, how hard
God had to stride.

Alone: Genesis

I will not abandon you;
I am determined to be
your mother. I adopt you,
press you into the pitch
of my body, absorb you
under my tongue.
I hear you cry out.
I close my mouth
and feel your scream
growing louder.
I clamp my jaws tight
until the blood I taste is my own.

We fall to the floor
together. We roll over each
other. We roll over and over
until our features merge,
our voices fall back
into our eye sockets.
I rock with explosion; smell
my chest, my thighs, my sex
ripping open. Your hands
swelling until they burst
the whole of my body.
We shower on each other
fragments; glue together
on the wooden floor.

I dig my heels in;
I am determined.
I call out your name
and your voice resounds
in the half-liquid
noise my tongue makes.
I call out your name
and you answer yes.
I ask if you are still
afraid, still waiting
to be reclaimed.
You answer, yes, yes.

I am determined to identify
myself, to identify you.
I start with my own nakedness.
I step out of it and hold it
arm's length from me. I probe it,
pull it to me, press my stomach
to it until my thighs ache.
I hold it to me
until it feels like hell.
I hold to it until
it feels like death,
until it feels like life,
until it feels like you.

For You, in the Darkness, Returning

Why have you come back?
And why have you brought him
with you? You deny it, but

I know you have hidden him
near. I smell him
in the shadows outside the window.
I smell him on your breath.
I cannot make love to you
with him watching. And he is,
the devil,
and he laughs at us.
He laughs at me in particular.
He knows I am impotent
in his presence.

Don't tell me the dead
don't want. Don't tell me
that's what being dead means.
This morning there were scratches
on the door, scratches on the couch.
I blamed them on the cat.
I accused my husband
who was also wounded but held silent.
He had scratches on his back.
I had claw marks the entire
length of my face. We covered
our eyes. We kissed and pretended
we were whole. We tried to believe
the blood was invisible.

After All Glory Has Passed before Us

On the last day
will some stranger still arise
early to dress in the black
garments of mourning, rereading
his prayer book? From the unknown
to us, will one still bow to kiss
the marble altar containing the bone
fragment of a saint, in our behalf?
On the last day
will six people offer to witness
and walk beside us and shoulder
us past the shrinking graves
of the lost, to our own name
chiseled in stone? On the last day,
as we kiss full on the mouth
and embrace for the final moment,

who will weep for our loss
and the next one and the one
after that? Who will still quiver
and fall to his knees, willingly
among the half-rotted apples
in the field? Who will profit
from the prayer and the kiss,
as the earth opens for us
and takes us in?

Kay Murphy

SIDNEY, ILLINOIS

Back Country Feminist Landscape

1

These patched mossy rocks by the shoreside—
I have been here before. Or them in me.
A dream of turtles, their backs gone
to fur. Deserted islands, or never lived on.
So this is why all the stillness,
you keeping to yourself like this,
settled in over your ears.

2

Mold waits for night to shine
or longer. Strange galaxy I step over
looking for something familiar. Lavender
starfish turn slick grey. The brain sprouts
hairs green as silk
that flourish behind the eyelids,
and you with your eyes wide open.

3

Insects swarm, always lose
their orbits for the craze of lights.
Wanting to be a star, spinning
into the dark, reappearing
punched out. The orders here:
Don't blink. Do not reveal your ambitions.

Patricia Hampl

ST. PAUL, MINNESOTA

This Is How Memory Works

You are stepping off a train.
A wet blank night, the smell of cinders.
A gust of steam from the engine swirls
around the hem of your topcoat, around
the hand holding the brown leather valise,
the hand that, a moment ago, slicked back
the hair and then put on the fedora
in front of the mirror with the beveled
edges in the cherrywood compartment.

The girl standing on the platform
in the Forties dress
has curled her hair, she has
nylon stockings—no, silk stockings still.
Her shoulders are touchingly military,
squared by those shoulder pads
and a sweet faith in the Allies.
She is waiting for you.
She can be wearing a hat, if you like.

You see her first.
That's part of the beauty:
you get the pure, eager face,
the lyrical dress, the surprise.
You can have the steam,
the crowded depot, the camel's-hair coat,
real leather and brass clasps on the suitcase;
you can make the lights glow with
strange significance, and the black cars
that pass you are historical yet ordinary.

The girl is yours,
the flowery dress, the walk
to the streetcar, a fried egg sandwich

and a joke about Mussolini.
You can have it all:
you're in *that* world, the only way
you'll ever be there now, hired
for your silent hammer, to nail pictures
to the walls of this mansion
made of thinnest air.

Hearth

You've seen those pictures
of the colonial hearth:
a black hook holding
the huge pot over the fire.
All the utensils were oversize,
the great wooden spoon as tall
as a woman in a starched cap,
the eternity of stirring.
I believe for a fact
the pot was never empty;
it never came off its hook,
why should it?
The hearth was huge,
a person could stand
inside the fireplace as if
it were a small hut, and warm.
Those people were smaller
than we can imagine,
we bend at their doorways.
In the dusty county museum
we hold their tiny, unreal shoes,
puckered like figs now
and not believable anymore.
We turn toward the hearth.
But what is the hearth
but a hook?

Jessie Kachmar

DES PLAINES, ILLINOIS

Our Mother the General

(On a news account of a prehistoric
tomb found in China of a woman commander
with retainers in full military regalia)

We have no word for female warlord
    She was (like Pharaoh) buried in a noble's crypt
        where favored dead were put away
           in gorgeous living trimmings

The burial mound hid her unbound feet
    that once rode against a Hun
        who cut her down and swept
           her daughters into sedan chairs

This Chinese woman had no written battle rules
    to hand over to unlettered Jean d'Arc
        surrounded finally
           only by her voices

Women queened the legend for a day—
    Penthesilea, a warrior at Troy
        with her one-breasted Amazons
           lively now as a maiden carved
                on a windjammer's bowsprit

The world is old, half-hidden in the folds of a fan

    Gentlemen awaiting the softness of women
        to drape an aura of violet around the world
           may continue waiting
Our mother asleep in hammered armor wears
        raiment authentic as any other

Paulette Roeske

EVANSTON, ILLINOIS

Dream of Trains

The Milwaukee Road dissects the town,
its whistle blending with dreams so a
woman forgets her waiting lover,
ready now after five years to
leave his wife. She forgets
and catches a quick train
to Paris, suitcase unlatching at will,
trailing lingerie.
So a child neglects his world
of apples, a nest in its branches,
the temptation of eggs, and turns
to face the train gathering itself,
his mother left on the platform,
lips moving, arms in the air.
So an old woman raises a jar of preserves
to the light, each strawberry
translucent and perfect on a warm day,
and sees the old country. Evacuation.
Sees her knees, cold as apples,
the wool skirt that wouldn't cover them
from eyes or the German winter.

A Little Drama

The wren house sways on its long pole
like another tree.
Father spits over his balcony. He's old.
He remembers the time a wren
died in the hole he cut too small
to admit its living body. It lodged
there limply, later swelling tight as a plug.
He climbed the ladder

hearing his heart in his ears.
It was that still.

He popped the body out with his stubby fingers
and tossed it in the slough
on limbs broken by the last storm.
The others know. Now they sit
on their shingled roof and rasp their little rage.
They fly somewhere else to sleep.

Snake in the Yard

It is probably innocent, traveling
across the stone path from rhubarb to squash
as best it can. I spring back
anyway. Father, with one thoughtless foot,
sends it flapping through the branches
of a stunted apricot.
Startled jays scatter; the snake
twists among them in the late sun.

I walk with quick steps back to the house,
carrying my fear. Father stays behind,
shading his eyes in the glare,
hoping to glimpse it
slipping uncrippled into the tall grass.

Going Under

Sierra Vista Hospital

The needle convinces me
to quit without a struggle.
In truth, there is little

I want to keep: the last time
with my lover, my daughter's honest eyes,
a moment of private glory. These
I hold like a few flowers
in a competent hand.

Then fingers loosen round the stems,
red and yellow blossoms drift
from the neat frame of vision. It is
so easy. Not nearly as arduous
as coming back to the full field
with neither choice nor right.

Alane Rollings

CHICAGO, ILLINOIS

Laws of Drifting

Philadelphia was fascinated by New Orleans
and New Orleans by things that bring on loss of memory.
It was my idea for us to go south, for you
to explain the Civil War.
I thought we'd make our furniture out of wood from the Gulf Coast,
that does not splinter, and make our bed
on the edge of my promises and your forgetfulness.
It was hot, and I put on too much perfume,
wrecked my stockings on hard rock, then fell asleep while you took in
the laws of migration and drifting.
As you liked to mutter when I faced the music,
"Well, you buttered your bread."
    I was good in the kitchen, too.
I wanted us to raise children and disappoint each other
as others do, but you managed to make it a test of friendship
when I spoke about the fall of Vicksburg.
You said to me, "Just look at yourself,"
wrapped me around your knees and gave me
the ambition to become respectable.
But I'm no good at simple things
and I'm afraid I was still sleeping
when you went up the lazy river without me.
    Now the streets are so full of affections
the go-go girls and scalawags are afraid to go to work.
Sailors keep me awake with their crewcuts and questions
or bring me down with belladonna from between the feet
of the large animals I kissed by mistake.
They tell me nothing has to happen, and I believe it,
but then I'm young. In the courtyards where they lost their figures,
overdue women wait for telegrams that say "OK, Baby," and don't come.
They tell me you've made a fortune in picnic tables
out of the timbers I'd been saving for my stake.
They're frightened of me and they're right.
Just look at me.

In the cafe where we played "Spite and Malice,"
I asked the waiter if he remembered which was our table.
He pointed to the corner and said, "I love you."
For such occasions I dress in flames
and bring my books on antidotes, my automatic writing board.
It's your life that comes shining at me like the answer,
but I'm busy every night.
None of them has your gift of runaround,
but I consider sending one of them to find you
and your somewhat enigmatic heart
and tell you I've forgotten you.
I'd say, "Why not? It's the end of a perfect day,"
but they know I only curse in public.
    We clairvoyants are more easily fooled,
and later I, too, will grow shining and silver and green,
and, as if I were short of slaves,
dance all night with good-looking thieves.

Janis Lull

CLEVELAND HEIGHTS, OHIO

The Seducer Steps Out, Just at Dusk

Your air, nice and legal,
Your lethal eye, your stare,
Arrested not, can't be impressed;
You never sweat. I do,
In the elevator with you.

Skin tones: you picture yourself in
Love tonight. You fall
Through hawk-space. I'm here,
By chance, for the drop, but not
The kill. This is my stop.

Sunset. Women, walking, lift
Their heads. You're in the air
By now. My life wants less
Jolt than you provide, but I
Remember things. Thanks for the ride.

Edith Freund

HIGHLAND PARK, ILLINOIS

A Woman of Style

One silent night before Easter
in the year of our Lord 1901
as dark fell on Russian peasants
as the Czar busied himself
with the Imperial egg
as Cossacks readied their horses and
their wine

Berte Rosenburg gathered up
the feather-quilts
tied them and wrapped
the required scarf around her golden hair
put three voluminous skirts on her person
tugged on her dead brother's knee boots
did not wait to say
goodbye to the Czar.

Berte Rosenburg native subject
to their royal majesties
the Czar and Czarina
took up a bundle to each hand
telling no one
allowing no hint to the wind
which blew through those villages
at that time.

Berte knew it sang too much—

in silence she disappeared
into the forest trees
into the mountain paths
up the old fold of the Urals
to where the crest breaks out of timberline.

Up over and down
to the younger side.

She walked always at night
ropes on the featherbeds bit into her hands
boots harried her skirts
wore away at her heels until
her flesh became hard as bootsoles
stiff as the backbone of
Berte Rosenburg.

Trusting no one but herself
she came at last to the sea
still carrying the featherbeds
as talisman to a future wedding
in case there should be no geese
in America.

Now seventy-nine years later
her granddaughter
dresses in voluminous skirts
pulls on high-fashion knee boots
ties her gold hair in a kerchief

never thinks of the Czar.

Handling It—

In ordinary houses
women sit
at kitchen tables
picking at the cloth
moving the heels of their hands
across the surface to gather
crumbs

while the person opposite says

Martha, your child has only
three months to live, Martha,
your husband
has run away with his mistress,
Martha, the mortgage is unpaid
and we will lose the farm

and the woman smoothes the cloth
runs her hand over it
gathering invisible toast crumbs
salt grains
into her cupped hands.

Caroline Knox

MILWAUKEE, WISCONSIN

Photo by Sarah Knox

Fresh Horses Should Be Waiting

The lady and
Julia try to
help with
the horses

Fresh horses should be waiting
for the tired riders and there should be oats
    and blankets, Julia,
for the sweating ones they leave; we must walk
    them
up and down and up and down—Oh God,
that's the boring part of horses, not the manure.

An
observation
period

Get the men a large kettle of water with dipper
    and ice;
their rugs and robes spread out very well on the
    ground.
Get them tiny brandy glasses with gold fruit
    pictured on them. Get them brandy.
We can lie down along the fringes now that
    it's dark
and stroke the backs of their arms while we listen
    to them sing.

The centuries
revisit them
unbidden

Children who sit quietly like us and read to you
    aloud
remind us of our Puritan forbears or who we would
    have been then
if we had sat thus by what Stevenson called "the
    cold candle"
and uttered little alphabets, a New England primitive
    in your own home.
It was peculiar that they had to wear hats in the house.

They look
for the
resolution

Dear Julia, you have always been such a comfort to me,
walking unembarrassed on every quadrant of the map.

Do You Traipse Long-Leggedly through Murky Woodlands

Do you traipse long-leggedly through murky woodlands?
You are such an Abercrombie-looking person
especially today in various grays and duns
and I am always taken aback by that sort of stuff.

This is not to say that I'm not your hearty
supporter because I am. I am just sort of
mystified, your mystique mystifies me
and I wish that when you were dishing out

municipal admonishments and info to the great unwashed
which is always your honor of course that
you were sending some neat special message
designed for me alone and me perennially

but you obviously aren't and it's very much better
as it is than as above which is all too goony.
These are occasions to pretend to overlook
and turn the gaze to figments of new constructs, perhaps in the snow,
        and squint dispassionately at their elevations

Alice Derry

WAUKEGAN, ILLINOIS

Letting Go

All night the rain's soft fists:
how deep does a bruise reach,
the soundings of one body
into another?

Eight years our words
like the skin-taut pellets
of raised knuckles.
Eight years our bodies
wore their places in the mattress:
even after we didn't mean it,
we crushed flesh to bone.

I am afraid to sleep
without you. As a child
probes the day's bruises,
my mind insists on our past:
last July, fireworks in the distance.
You grabbed my arm: look at the field.
Hundreds of fireflies flamed,
paused and flamed,
as if it were day,
as if the whole meadow had bloomed.

These Hills, Mother

Summers I come back to them.
From the air their brown bush like velvet,
trimmed by the Snake's one satin line.

I want to watch again
how they fall to the river
in textures of prickly pear and thistle,
gravel and poison sumac; how their springs
seep through Ponderosa, swell the Snake.
It returns no green.

Like my dream where our bones were pressed
into one flesh: too little for both of us,
the twenty years I lived in this valley.

You know too that wind flattens
cheat grass at the top, lichen
works its painstaking needlepoint
across the outcroppings. You know
how the hills fold into each other at twilight,
secretly, as a woman does,
how we've never really touched.

I return every summer to dream
of the hills, feel their sparse weave
beneath my fingers. On the porch after supper
I place this rough-knit shawl around you
against the evening's chill.
The comfort of familiar cloth
between us: you know its weight;
I, its roughened grain.

Judy Little

CARBONDALE, ILLINOIS

Melting

All responsible winters collect snow.
High places accumulate themselves, and their white
      weight
Sags till the overgrown icefield oozes
Blue-bulged like exposed brains knotted with excess
      of dreams—
Glaciers bent on planetary reformation.

Their years of hardened snow remake the world.
A stiff crest of ice heaves forward
And grinds all trapped history
Into the slowly splitting canyons.
It spreads thickened in the center by a ridge of
      bruised rubble
And slopes to the sea, the ice like a blunt petal
Dirtied with the mountains it has dragged away.

Tourists on sunny decks wait for the collapse.
The ship shudders by
And the empty eye of a camera opens
On the rumble of ice-dust
A solid snowload crumbling to blue powder
The freed ice-chunks melting on the green sea.

The engines grind northward
And the wake of the summer ship gathers the long
      sun.
The icebergs eddy
On banners of lagging light and drown.

The sleepers inside turn as the engines
Tug and plunge
But the heart is on vacation.

It halts and shudders again and then shrugs off
The weight of winter
Dream by thundering dream.

Television News

My first shot president
My first coffee-break massacre
First blood wide-screened for family-rooms
First burning child's eye-witness face
First scream's exclusive microphone
First poll's first sample of my first
      Legal blood's final opinion
First hero's first explosion of first
      Hand and first arm and first heart
First taste's last tongue's first tortured meat
First white hand shaking first dark crotch
First reporter's first conscience first
      Gainfully employing net truth
First disaster-prone history in
      Recorded screen proclaimed broadened
      Media truced supreme calendar's
      Court date Christmas according to
      Authoritative privilege first
      Leaked Thursday unedited snaps
      Public source for interview first;

The zenith war, a cornered fire,
Winked its schedule of daily words,
And stood in tune against the wall;
It revolutionized error;
When the city burned—the gray voice proved—
Some people were found at home in the fire.

Divorce

There was just a step to get into
And we had learned to approach a convention of
     hallways
Or greet a performance of doors
And actually pass out smiles
And carry the groceries of mortal conversation
Even offering politely
To answer each other's weather

  (We held back only what might have taken us
   From one hour to the next—
   We might have graced an intermission
   Scheduled for a velvet matinee)

All of a nowhere the sudden
A split half second can
Fall like the sky

For instance hunger
And the errands one is likely to run into
Especially at night
Such as passing each other in a double-crossed
     eyebeam
And the automatic door flings the stars open

  (If exits are such sweet sorrow
   Why should a handful of yesterday's light
   Startle the throat like sand?)

Therese Becker

LAKE ORION, MICHIGAN

Geese in Fog

I

Like still thoughts they sit,
mounted on the earth,
drawing the darkness inside them,
their wings folded tight
beneath listening bodies,
as if earth had a heart
that beat only in fog,
that beat only in silence and waiting.

Geese move and shift the thick air,
connecting their casual postures—
a portrait of passage.
Long necks bend backward
to the warmth of the body,
as a curve of thought homing
to the song in their spine.

II

A man with a camera chases perceptions
that roll like fog
along the low flat back of the land,
that roll like fog
into that space that captures
the birds of our lost perception.

Beergarden Photo

This photograph is a message
won't stay in the album
wants to shed darkness here
in the sunlight
on this kitchen table
the faces are nervous
because the faces behind them
won't stop talking

the people in the photo
belong to the child
the child belongs to no one
she is afraid of the glasses
ice never melting
thirst never ending
the pouring of silence

the man in the uniform
carries a grenade in his heart
the woman holds the child between them
so she cannot move
her breath is waiting
for the uniform to take
the man back
the man that belongs to the child
back to another war

the relatives are supposed to be there
looking like relatives
smiling their shuffleboard smiles
it is right after all
this photo will always smell
like a beergarden
play like a juke box forever

69

Lorene Erickson

LIVONIA, MICHIGAN

Virginia

Virginia, the youngest,
was saved by a Baptist preacher
who spoke to her
in tongues so sweet
her thighs melted

causing the Reedy Creek to rise,
the West Virginia mud
sucking her ankles,
the water lapping her calves,
the holy ghost floating

her all the way
to Michigan
and the ward for unwed mothers
where the bawling gift
was named
and given up
to Lucy, her Christian sister.

Father Unknown
grew practical,
farmed a dairy,
and at forty his heart closed up
like a tiny fist.

Virginia
rode the return ticket
to Reedy undercurrents,
cowmired,
married Gault the postman.

Each year's baby
washes out of her like gravel.
The creek is chest high now.
She has cast bread upon the waters;
it will not come back.

The Outing

She had the children
all dressed
when she left the house.

I watched her fasten
the red knitted cap
on the little one
squirming under her touch,
the older one turning in circles.

Those poor little fish.

What a squawking of gulls
she must have heard
as she raised their bodies
high over the railing
of the South Street Bridge.

What thin line snapped
as she cast them like bobbers
to sink and rise and sink again,
the red one the brightest
against the black Schuylkill.
skykill

What fisherman, what friend,
what host of passion
did she believe was waiting
that she, too, must join,

her skirt spreading
in the air like a net.

You Look

you look at him
with the love you look
at him with the love in my eyes

you touch him
with my fingers you touch him
feel his heat as he leans

you lick your tongue in the curve
of his throat   I taste the salt

he does not know
it is me he breathes
he sees another body   yours
your hair nesting his hands

when you press him to your breasts
your belly   press his head
between your legs   he remembers
he remembers only the dark moment
knows only his own cells spinning

we are not a part of him
we are the hundred hands stroking
the eyes looking

Alice Ryerson

CHICAGO, ILLINOIS

Woe One

The play she's in has no central character.
People enter
put books on shelves
empty ashtrays
blow their noses and exit.
Bit parts
they leave her stage
for more exhilirating employment.

There's no plot either
though the off-stage thunder
makes promises and the stage-set
was made by a Master.

Woe Two

An old elephant
stranded alone
on a far shore
waving her trunk
at the gray backs
far away
in reeds beyond water.

Woe Three

Passing through the castles of anger,
she becomes sour and dangerous,
a green apple bewitched.

Cruel, a glass sherd
glinting in sweet jelly.

Vindictive, a snake stepped on
while going harmlessly about its business.

Insatiable, all mouths,
open and empty.

Sick with loss, smelling
of decaying leaves and self-pity.

In the country of anger
she is different and dying,
alone and unlike,
split away from the others . . .

unique, like all the rest of them
who are out there and still moving.

Helen Winter

SKOKIE, ILLINOIS

Tradition

In the foyer, this modern temple
displays antiques for visitors,
ancestral rituals, frozen, in a little museum.
Friday evening, I can respond
to brief, arid prayers.
Here I could be honored, called to the altar.
No daily morning service takes place.
No phylacteries lie on members' foreheads.
Leather thongs never wind around their arms.
When the Sabbath ends, they do not smell
aromatic spices in an ornate box.

Entering an orthodox synagogue,
enticed by the warmth of tradition,
I am excluded, a nothing.
Only men don phylacteries on secular days,
handle spices and light tapers
at the close of holy rest.
Women only watch from a balcony.
If I am not satisfied by relics under glass,
I may listen to men reading the law,
draping prayer shawls I cannot drape,
and thanking God they were not born a woman.

Maxine Silverman

SEDALIA, MISSOURI

Meditations on the Body: Right Hand

How the veins branch around the knuckles
interests me—the pale rivers and the range,
the peninsulae of fingers.

And how cold or fatigue bring
the faint deep aching
where the bones joined force again.
Flex. Rub.
Tend the old wound, the body's memory
of flying from the horse's bare back into a linden.
Learning the impossibility of a fist,
learning to knead with the left hand,
to love myself awkwardly, then well enough.

The self aches that way, too,
a body of memories
of sudden flying and blows that do not kill,
but teach the stunning lessons:
how little is needed
and how much of that.

Movements on a Theme

1
To stand out in relief against the visible.
To claim the simple movement from talk
into silence
as when a woman
removing herself from company to a window
draws the curtain.

She is found at last
staring out across the planes
of evening
light,
of darkness,
and when asked what she is about
murmurs *nothing*
        getting ready
to return.

2
The road is not long enough
today. She wants to walk and walk.
She likes the sweat sliding down the deep bed
of her spine
and between her breasts, likes how
it tastes on her lip
and the movement of her tongue bringing it in

and her bones swinging back and forth
like gates or knives.
She hates the house growing larger,

its white bulk crouched and blinding with its white
        paint.
She flings the screen door back
against the shingles hard
and her shoes can't sufficiently break the carpeted
        silence
as she stomps down the hall
wishing this were winter
wishing this were ice.

3
She cannot bear her hair any longer
on her shoulders. Desire,
the enactment of hope, she bundles
in a tight green band at the nape.

No
a *tenor* sax
        someone in another apartment
she is not sure where
The melody clears the courtyard
in the late morning air
She improvises some steps
straining to follow   this clean line

Isn't this how it always is?
From somewhere
unexpected
often before she knows she wants

music

the way healing can be recorded
as it occurs
though how it begins and why
remain unknown
            essentially mysterious
            the body living out its code
and she dances,
her hair loosens
with the movement of her head
and arms.

Miriam Pederson

GRAND RAPIDS, MICHIGAN

The Quickening

My dresses can no longer hide
the size of me
stares at my belly
are more frequent
undisguised
I buy milk and fruit
read novels in the park
gaze through branches on trees
at cloud joining cloud
there is someone living inside me
I tell my friends
they think I'm crazy
this has happened since time began
why the surprise
but this is different
no one lived inside me before
no one kicked or swam about
in my belly before this
if you ask me it's supernatural
my husband laughs a lot these days
he watches me
as I disappear around the corner
in the car or on my bicycle
he waters the lawn too much
and picks the roses
before they are ready to bloom

Erosion

Everything is wearing thin
the rugs   the dish towels
our socks   this chair
the snow
look at it
worn and soiled
it's a crime
to let things go this far
nothing can be done
to bring them back
who can remember
when patches on jeans
were important
my mother
turned collars on shirts
to make them new again
but that is over
there is no time
to save things anymore
I am afraid to bear a child
with this thinness all around
sheets that tear
when we toss in the night
hair that falls
from our heads
top soil that washes
from our land
who can know
when these shoes will wear out
and my child will walk barefoot
over what is left

Gloria Still

FORT WAYNE, INDIANA

Summer Storm, Highway 37

lightning/cavern/zero
visibility/barefoot
child asleep beside me
trust the weather

trust the worn unbalanced tire
trust the steering/trust
the speeding trucks
trust the wind

trust the radiator thermostat
the gas gauge/the
headlights/trust
the heart/you already know

the decent reactions/the
art that precedes loving
and living apart
pull off the road

trust the dark/eyes
of the man who shines/through this
thunderhead/on his
separate way to the mountains

trust that gypsy
light/the wet
stars/the tambourine he shakes
against the windows

Jill Breckenridge

MINNEAPOLIS, MINNESOTA

Attitudes of Thanksgiving

Last winter, everything iced over:
houses, streets, desire, even mild
affection. Our talk trailed off

into snow flurries, our Monet painting
of water lilies froze white on white.
You and I curled up in our cold
separate lives, drifted into deep
slumber, occasionally reaching out
in the dark, but seldom touching.
In this climate, winter kills.

It also ends, and, like the last survivor,
I take nothing for granted. April,
the world is about to be born again,
and this time I'll be there to see it.
Impatient for green leaves, the hallelujahs
of tulips, I walk to the lake
without a coat. Shivering, I feel the sun
on my face. Bathsheba, our black dog,
looking neither up nor down, trots
through broken bottles of Miller's and Hamm's,
danger with no warning smell. Canada geese
stand awkwardly courting on the spongy ice.

You look at me like I am that garden
greening behind the thorned hedge—
I accept your royal gifts and again
dream in color. Later, waking, we recall
dark winter mornings, as our bodies
melt into attitudes of thanksgiving.

Pamela Painter

CHICAGO, ILLINOIS

Photo by Robie Macauley

My Own Good

You have told me for my own good:
how the world has edges; how roads
narrow in the distance into lines; how cross-roads
have a way of pulling limbs from heart.

I have retreated from the branch
to you, but it was the fall I wanted,
the needle's silk under my back,
my chances never broken by the sky.

I have acted for my own good.
Your voice the edge I couldn't sail beyond,
the lime in my palm, the current
going down, not across as those you sail.

Your caution tamped shut my pores, closed
my feet, entered like silt into my hair,
till I saw good for what it was.
I am across the edge that isn't there.

Martha Friedberg

CHICAGO, ILLINOIS

Photo by Chip Miller

Father

When dreams of a live wife
swam in your arms,
you would reach for us
and touch our cheeks to test the flesh.
Yes, we survive.

Children, you'd bellow:
keep your bowels open. Don't eat trash.
We nibbled in secret
and grew in the dark
like bulbs in the basement
till you spun us around in the light.
Nobody failed. And nobody passed.

Years you are gone.
We still tremble.
But what do I care?

Father, you were a beauty.
Four times you voted for FDR.

Nancy McCleery

LINCOLN, NEBRASKA

Photo by Walt Hays

The Rag Lady

Like a witch with one foot
in the Black Forest
she wades "O" Street
dragging mud and mushrooms
from dark regions into our town

From behind flat lensed glasses
she is too occult to notice
how with the look of an unbeliever
I take her in
how I see her in 80 degree weather
covered layer upon layer
in black with a sash
gushing red to her waist

Under her blouse
I think she has three breasts
and a mirror in which she
is the fairest

She is bent over
pushing a cart filled with rags
moving it down the street
as if Hansel and Gretel
were in there
perhaps a pot of some
ancient ointment

Moving along the street now
in deep undergrowths and thickets
she chews gum lifting a transistor radio
to her ear as if charming herself away:
a black ship breaking in dark waves

Claire's Braids

The woman knows how it's done,
having learned from childhood
to weave with long grass

the right then the left
over the middle strand.
At first as loose as a cobweb,

later tidying up her hair
against wind and dust
in tight straight braids.

Now seventy, she says her brains
are in her fingers, and shows
the finished rug

she's been working on two winters,
gathering a lifetime
for this one

she thinks her last. No plans
laid out at the beginning, she looked
to make sense of her places by taking

to her rugs the color of the Poudre River,
the sky above Boston Knob, green firs,
remembering how they dipped in the rain,

Indian paintbrush riding among buttercups,
wild asters and roses near thistles,
wild currants growing from rocks.

She goes about it slowly, strokes
the balls of wool as she takes them down
from sunroom walls and ceilings

where they hang in baskets:
shades of night stars, agate,
clouds at sunrise, thunderheads.

She plaits the wind in cross currents with rock
from above the timber line, eyes the color
of the stream, then looks to the woods,

the aspen,
how they lean
together in threes.

Jeanine Hathaway

WICHITA, KANSAS

Photo by Hugh Tessendorf

Two Steps Forward

Down to the well
the woman carries her
vessel carved
with animal shapes,
rampant, huddled,
astir with a memory vague
as bees around a dead log,
a blurred hum of memory
of how it was before the human
animal became separate, singular,
absent minded. Further back
of how they all were once
water creatures: splashing woman
and splashing lion in a cold flip
of scales and flat eyes,
that phantom strangeness of no legs
or paws when this desert
earth was thick with seaweed
ripe and breathless. Now the woman,

hairy and dry, their distant sister,
returns to water, returns them all
to water.

Grandmother God

You delivered land out of water, settled
horizons radiant with variety and the need
for legs. It was then you knew time, flash,
the glint of something turning perhaps away.

With ears like petals or wings
you listen now for your early comfort,
the voice you found singing your name.
Although the dark has thinned,
gone vague with shadows, is not what
you would recall—although your name is
quiet, Grandmother God, you are aware
of that old hum
dissatisfaction
rising again like a resource.

Faye Kicknosway

BLOOMFIELD HILLS, MICHIGAN

Cassandra

Do you know pain?
Are you the nightingale, the cloth
of darkness, singing?
Listen: I am the radiance the dark
moves through; I am its speech,
it is trapped in my tongue,
my weeping. Beware;
I am ashes, ruined.

Who is to say what is stronger?
What is done by the hand
or what lingers after the hand
withdraws?
Prophecy watches and laments.
To act and see only
the act
is blindness.

What heart is more pure than mine?
I am shown here in blood; but it is
deception. Death has tricked me.

I do not speak wildly, neither do I
excuse any part of what I say.
It is death I hear, robing himself,
his sweet, red voice joyful.
He ties his hair back from his face.
He is radiant; the air thickens around him;
look, he is like fire.

I do not want to see what is hidden
in the air,
what moves it

and almost steps through it.
I do not want to have it look at me,
speak to me; I could foretell it, I could fear
it into shape.
Why speak?
I might distract it from happening.
I am dominated by dreams;
why tremble?
Why say one word?

Brothers, Father, friends;
I am the monster; I have escaped.
I am fallen over; there is no wetness
to me, no heat.
Even in the afternoon, when the roof tiles
swoon and the streets are fetid
and hot, I am cold and dry
and collapsed upon myself.

The man who brought me here thought:
"I will catch her,
understand her, the secret, bitter
odor.
Why so pitiful? So constant?
Her hair flies, wonderfully sweet.
I will risk it, whisper to her mouth;
I will catch her."

He was caught, swallowed up.
Never had there been a body
more pleasing,
nor a time. Dark, his heavy legs,
the smoke

his breathing made in the air,
he lifted himself, fixed himself
in my eyes, amazed, unremitting.
Blinded and bumping into things,
he pushed his way outside.

He was caught; a shape had risen
and trembled about him in his dream.
Its touch woke him.

There was light in the courtyard;
bells sounded beyond the wall.
A wind blew in the yard
and he could not walk out into it.
There was another death
crouched among the dead.
Why did everything seem still?

Today, There Is Love

She had not planned it;
there were the dishes,
her insomnia,
and a moth above the kitchen sink.
Everything was quiet.
Her image in the kitchen drain
fascinated her, how it got there,

her face, the size
of a teaspoon,
looking up.

This is only the first chapter.
It is her standing at the door,
wishing he were standing there
instead.
She has her mouth pulled down, sour.

How capable of love he seems;
how grey he looks. Flowers

throw themselves into the air,
wanting to be eaten, to be ecstatic
and touched all over.

She resists his speaking,
draws back from him, dissatisfied,
breathless.

In the dark,
he talks in her hair.

His voice is moist.
He is shoulders and hips
and contains all the plants of the earth
inside his flesh.

He has a face like a saw.
She feeds him pudding.
He thinks of all the fruit he's eaten,
is bored, distracted,
brushes crumbs from his moustache.

When he is wrapped in his sheet,
he says he is hollow,
words are flies and their buzzing
is painful.
He slaps his skin, but can't reach them.
Their wings, their legs;
he has no internal organs.

She dreams the same dream;
it is a funny dream.
Everything is metal or cloth.

She feels that, any moment, God
will enter the room.
She will recognize Him by His tall
boots, His toothpick,
by the way change rattles in His
pocket. He will ask her for directions
and look distracted
until she gives them.

She is awake and silent.
There is a shape in the urgent
night; she has touched it; its clumsy,
strange hands
have touched her.

Pigeons, on the telephone wires,
on the roof's eaves, sleep.
What captured thing is free?
What smoothly cold and latticed thing
touches and changes her?
There is a smell of hyacinth, an odor thick
and full of sorrow
in the room.

Carol Barrett / Anita Skeen

WICHITA, KANSAS

Interiors

How large is a house?

> wide enough for the floor
> to stretch its boards from east to west,
> tall enough for rafters
> to speak at night with the stars

Where do candles belong?

> in far corners, like stars

What is the most important spice?

> one that is always absent,
> its empty container staring down
> from the second shelf like the only star
> in the midsummer sky

How is gingham made?

> from the squares of silence

When does a house die?

> when the only sound it hears
> is itself

What is kept in a trunk?

> things too fragile
> for the sharp light
> of day

When is the clock wrong?

> when it brings on the night
> before i am ready,

> when it lets it escape
> before i am done

How long is a blanket soft?

> until all its history is washed
> away, till it is stretched on a rack
> in the noon sun

How do you know your room in the dark?

> by the sound of its breathing,
> the way it lies down
> at night to sleep

What do you take on a trip?

> things i have been saving for
> some time: addresses of friends
> i used to know,
> a shirt i've never worn,
> the book i've meant to read
> all year, the need
> to leave

Why do you breathe?

> to know i am alive,
> so my room will know me in the dark

What sound do you listen for?

> the sound of trees walking
> in the forest at night, their soft branches
> sweeping together the stars,
> and the deep breathing
> of the mountains as they sleep on
> undisturbed

Anita Skeen

WICHITA, KANSAS

In the Field, Treasure

(for Carol Konek)

She was a lover of primary sources:
rock, wheat, bone,
mirrors of red, leafy plants
eaten as vegetables, ripe lemons,
blueprints for the lives of displaced women.
She was visitor to such local wonders
as Blue Hole, Garden of Eden,
the Pringle Tree. She wished to meet
the woman who rode with the last cattle drive,
the secretary who pummeled the keys
of the first Royal, the guru in Boulder
who (her friend told her) was an international
jewel thief. Her searches were like drawing
water from a good well.

She studied their lives for rough drafts,
noted what words they tried to erase, why
their punctuation changed.
She spent hours reading
footnotes, cursing careless documentation,
wanting to know who struck fire
to the first tallow, who last saw the dodo
waddling around Mauritius Island,
who sat in the rocker
before Whistler's mother,
who was the first woman to save her village
from the floodtide, the first
to carve her name in runes.

For Susan, Turning Thirty

This November, the brown leaves
will sweep across empty intersections
in these early morning hours
as they have for years, as they did
when we waited for schoolbuses, pumpkin
and cider in the air, or on those southern
mountain mornings when frost needled our paths
to the main road.

Last night, when I said I had known you
for twenty-five years, I grew older
than our first grade teacher, lumbering
through the chalk-filled sunlit room in white
anklets and oxfords. The twins,
an English teacher called us, as we circled
in identical orbits, mine always with
imperfections, just slightly off-course.
I looked in mirrors hoping
you would look back;
I was Castor, you Pollux.

Years later, you are still
the protagonist in my dreams:
your face replaces that of the woman
I stand next to you, you sit in my classroom,
you are with me in blizzards, car wrecks,
at the opposite end of the green felt table
in smoke-filled rooms.
We are customers watching
a grocer weigh bologna, and I turn
to ask you, "Are rock lyrics poetry?"
If you are not there,
I am searching.

We are each other
even now: I feel my hand
lift a glass at your table.
The dolls I buy are for your daughters.
I have fled to Kansas and you have moved
into my old territory, a few houses
from my house. The heavens spread
between us. Now we are differences:
our choice of partners, the way
we dress, the books that change
our lives. I could not write this poem
for myself, turned thirty
in September. Once again,
it is for you, it is for me.

Susan Hauser

PUPOSKY, MINNESOTA

How, Like This Spring, Slowly

How, like this spring, slowly
I rise from the long steel winter.

Today driving past
the funeral home,

I saw myself walking
in that door. And I remembered

I did not dress you.
I am sorry for that.

I was glad
when you were born to

bare your torso,
feel each foot

and hand, to touch
your pouch,

to bring your wet mouth
the river of my breast.

I told the man
I wanted to dress you.

He said no. I did not argue,
did not want to feel

your skin turned to stone,
to bone,

to not bend
in the water of my arms.

Like the spring slowly
I rise from the long steel winter.

In my dreams you are often
lost. In these words I

dress you now,
sweet Aaron,

your wildflower face,
these word-wings from my fingers

folding around
your willow bones.

Slow as spring,
the spirit-milk rises.

Bring your wet mouth.

Naomi Long Madgett

DETROIT, MICHIGAN

Twice a Child

(for my mother at ninety)

Butterflies fan fragile, filmy wings
in the darkening forest I lead her through,
holding her hand, guiding her trembling
footsteps, buttoning her memory
as I used to dress my dolls
when she was mother and I
was child.
Now overhanging leaves
filter fading gold through shadow
to the damp and slippery ground beneath
as she drifts through the twilight
of a fairy tale whose characters' names
she has forgotten.
And I can only guess what distant bells
she hears tolling
at the top of the hill she climbs
on all fours.

Judith Minty

NEW ERA, MICHIGAN

Photo by Robert Turney

Dancing the Fault:
The Poetry of Judith Minty

BY SHIRLEY CLAY SCOTT

As "Christine on Her Way to China" demonstrates, the subject of Judith Minty's poetry is her biography: family, friends, husband, daughters, temporary dislocations in New York or California, and perennial, atavistic returns to her "heartland," Upper Michigan. Many of her poems simply try to realize the facts of her biography, to apprehend in words the full emotional inflections of the "briefest shifts and passings" of her experience—in the way a painter might try to capture the exact color values of a landscape at a certain hour or of a still life in a certain light. In such poems the voice is reflective but open and conversational. The lines relax on the page; there is time for the image and the apposition it begets or the explanation it requires: "I saw bolts of lightning explode from the black silk, / I felt something break, a sunburst."

There are other poems, more hermetic, cryptic, disjunctive, in which she is not merely trying to know the facts of her experience but "trying to remember" something prior, interior and uncertainly related to her biography, something whose existence she deduces largely from her consciousness of its absence, from her sense that she once possessed or was possessed by it.

In "Trying to Remember" her gnomic expression for this fugitive something is "what my grandmother told me" and her imagistic approximation of it is a "humming," perhaps the humming she heard one particular time as a child of four or five when she sat on her grandmother's lap. "We were both half- / asleep. She was humming, I think. The breath of her love on my arm." The architecture of this poem, which brings into quiet, moving colloquy brief meditations on her correspondence with a woman she trusts and with whom she can create "another

woman," vignettes of her longing for the man with whom she can "fly back to the body," and memories of that summer afternoon, suggests that her project in love and in language is to recover "the humming" that haunts but eludes her. "I was so close to her heart then, her fingers pulsing / over my arm. . . . I am trying to remember what my grandmother told me."

We may, rather inadequately, call this something that she is "trying to remember" a pristine sense of the self. (Her own images—"another woman" she can sometimes create in confidence with a friend, or the state of being released in bodily love, or simply a "humming"—are richer phrasings.) And we may turn to her earlier poems to find that the components of that self are simple and common enough— mother and father; death and desire; water and wilderness. Out of these terms and their press upon one another she must make a poetry and a self.

Mother and father are presences throughout Minty's work. The intricately made title poem of *In the Presence of Mothers* elucidates the actual and metaphorical significance of the mother. Running through the poem is the pun on *la mer, la mere*. Also there, but submerged, is the further Latinate pun on *mare* (sea) and *amare* (love) and *amārē* (bitingly, poignantly). Biology links the mother to the unconscious processes of the natural universe: "squall lines, laboring, / roll one on the other / out from the island." Human consciousness of what she nurtures and loves and relinquishes to those processes links the mother to an almost deific awareness of grief:

> Silence of cold, a falling
> of tears. Still

arms lift out of ice:
the sorrow of it,
the loss.

And because the human *would* know and the poet *would* name the grief, the mother is indirectly linked to the daughter's urge to seek out the biting knowledge that separates human consciousness from the mindless laboring of nature:

Black into light and back
the sun rises and falls in its tedium.
But the delicate stars,
they nurse us
along the moon's yellow path
into hard arms, new openings.

The "hard arms" and "new openings" are masculine images of embrace and penetration which derive from the father, the engenderer. "My Father's Watch" from *Lake Songs* identifies the father with desire and with the self that finds its source in desire. There is a confirmation of self in reciprocated desire:

Bath clean in my nightgown,
I stood waiting for his sigh.

. . . .

"Where's my girl?"
I'd run into his arms,
into his beard's rough stubble.

The hard things that he has to teach are the lessons of time. He is associated in Minty's poems with a gold watch and the nightly ritual of winding it and gazing into its face until, late in his life, she sees it "burn" in his hand. But the countervailing knowledge he has is of the north country. He will be the poet's guide into the wilderness of the Yellow Dog River where redress for loss may be found.

Death informs all the books. Drownings stun and maim the girl at water's edge in *Lake Songs and Other Fears*; deaths by cancer and suicide, by mean old age and nature's caprice rend the woman on another shore writing [the newly completed manuscript] "Letters to the Snow Country." And desire manifests itself, from her early poems on, in imagery of light or fire and wildness. In "The Horse in the Meadow" (*Lake Songs*) the horse is an archetypal figure for the onset of desire:

I saw him, that wild stallion,
when I dressed in white. He
galloped along our ridge at dusk
ran against the sky's flame,
mane and tail streaming
fine strands before dark clouds.

"Prowling the Ridge" from *In the Presence of Mothers* finds the young woman as wife "burning" for her husband's dream and for the untamed wolf she imagines him to be in that dream. And, as a woman at mid-life in "Trying to Remember," she knows the fresh return of desire when "the coyote eyes" of her lover "glitter" and "a wolf rises up through [her] bones."

The basic images are organized as mythic progenitors in the poems. Desire complicates itself with death. Two poems from *Lake Songs*, which the poet locates in her tenth year, imagine that the oncoming of sexuality was a kind of death and that sexuality and death are inextricable knowledges. In "Lake Michigan" the water is not "La mere" but a masculine, even animal, lover with whom she colludes.

I drowned here when I was ten,

. . . .

felt arms cradle me, no longer
cried for mother, was sucked into black sleep.

. . . .

I strip off my clothes,
fall into the waves. I will
go deep, let it lick my skin,
feel its pulse as we sink together again.

And "Flight of the Eagle" associates her tenth summer and a "trembling" vigil to see an eagle fly as "gold burned on his feathers" with her father's coming for the girl "through heat waves, / wearing a band of mourning."

These earlier poems indicate that it is the intuition of death that first served to inform desire. "From his nest, the eagle answered my cry." But later poems suggest that an awareness of death inhibits desire, tames it, or takes it captive. The wild stallion that the girl in white saw "then" is "now" a horse in the meadow; even in this tame form, he is menaced by an old crone in black [the movement toward death] who wants to "climb on him, break him, ride him back to her house." (The Horse in the Meadow,

Lake Songs) And the wolf prowls the ridge in the *husband's* dream from which the conscious wife is shut out. (Prowling the Ridge, *In the Presence of Mothers*)

As the girl becomes woman, the menace of death intimidates her, blocks desire, cuts her off from the "humming" she needs as woman and as poet. "Hawk" is a compelling portrayal of that state. In the dead hawk that "even the cats won't touch" she knows her own cruel fate.

> I feel worst about the feet
> hanging from the backporch beam—
> fists clenched, claws like my own hand
> holding the knife.

In the hawk that flies over the mutilated remains of its mate, she sees herself: incomplete, keening, neither recognized nor recognizing, far removed from the child who sat close to her grandmother's heart.

But both mother and father have provided images to which the thwarted woman has recourse. In "Making Music," the last poem of *Lake Songs*, the mother is half-animal, half-artist. She sits in "the cave" of the basement "like an organist," a "flash of fur under her arm" as she feeds damp sheets into an iron mangle, her "instrument," and draws "clean hymns" out of the roller. But the daughter claims she has "no talent for music," is "not mother." And she is right. An image of biology links the mother to process. The daily routine that absorbed and comforted the mother is one from which the daughter has been extricated by consciousness. The daughter's music, if it is to be at all, cannot be "clean hymns" of the "dampness of muslin" and the smell of "soap under scorch," but music which names what *she* knows. And what she knows is too much death. Its maiming thump interrupts the "humming" and leaves her the static, not the current, of desire.

> Headlights rest on the fur of dead animals, and
>   my wheels
> roll over them: rabbits, cats, squirrels
> pressed into the sheet of the highway. It is a long
>   drive home.
> The hum of the motor blends with the thumps
>   of bodies
> and the static rock beat out of the radio.

How then to harness the energy of the animal (the flash of fur) to the needs of the poet? The father has taught her the way north, to the Yellow Dog River, and when in desperation she follows him there, she is able to tap that energy and to bring it back through adult consciousness that has been chastened by its knowledges and chagrined by its losses and failures. So constrained, animal energy becomes transformative power available to woman *and* poet. The *Yellow Dog Journal* is distinguished writing; the images are sharp and clear, the poems are small but certain of themselves, and the concluding section is marked by moments of lyric grace.

In fall when the daughter takes her father's route north, she begins to slough off her woman's skin and twenty years of being "planted" in the suburbs, and she arrives her "father's child" in *his* land, *his* shack on the riverbank, "the Yellow Dog barking home to [Lake] Superior." (Fall, 1) She finds her father's slippers "now mine to wear," discovers him a "barely muffled" presence in the cabin and remembers that *he* taught her desire, wildness, and access to the self.

> It was he told me the Yellow Dog
> made my sleep spin into the woods, to the falls
> above the clearing, the ore shining gold in the sun.
> Late nights, he'd whisper its bends,
> my face close to his Finnish guttural,
> cheeks flushed from his beard's rough stubble.
>
> (Fall, 10)

In this place of his, she finds proof that she *is*:

> Thinking how good it is
> to come up the path from the river,
> chimney smoke sifting above the trees,
> to open the cabin door and find myself
> still there, stirring logs in the stove.
>
> (Fall, 12)

In this place of his, she can decipher and accept the hints of the challenges and devastations yet to come:

> Tonight on the porch,
> I unbutton my shirt, let my breasts
> swim in the full moon's light.
>
> (Fall, 13)

She can let the "bear" who has stalked her dreams (and her poems) since childhood invade her until she repeats as an adult what she first experienced as a child of ten; she knows now the full implications of what she intuited then. And this time she does not allow herself to be sucked into "black sleep." (Lake Michigan, *Lake Songs*) She grows wild herself, so that she can take in death and release it as desire, desire that knows.

> I am digging a grave, three feet by one.
> It could hold a child or an animal
> . . . .
> . . . I step away from the hole.
> Never looking over my shoulder,
> I roll back on these haunches
> And let the long shrill howl rise.
> It runs out like a song from my throat.
>
> (Fall, 29)

This theme is explicated further in "Trying to Remember," particularly in the passage in which the woman experiences a fresh return of self-articulating desire. Her hand inadvertently touches the man's hand on a knife handle. The knife in this poem, as in "Hawk," is an image of the biting knowledge of death that is, for Minty, inextricably bound with desire. When wildness comes in aid of desire, as it does here, "his coyote eyes glitter, a wolf rises through my bones," and the ecstasy is a knowledge that subsumes and answers death.

When in "Spring" she comes again to the river, the hermit thrush [marked forever by Whitman as the bird of death and desire] "opens his throat" and her own lines "flow over the page." She is not, now, far from that long-ago summer afternoon:

> the afternoon sun
> warms my shoulders, my back
> in its slow circle.
>
> (Spring, 9)

Upstream she even finds a place by her "father's sandy beach" where the sound of the wild Yellow Dog becomes the full-bodied hum of "a contented woman."

> This water flows, then catches
> in little eddies, almost
> trying to run upstream again.
> Then it hurries on, tugs
> at the bush next to me,
> nods the twig at the bend.
> It plays the same at the falls,
> only louder, with a certain fury.
> Here, by my father's sandy beach,
> the river is surely a contented woman.
>
> (Spring, 18)

Such a breakthrough to the self and to poetry is not permanently granted. Wildness is not always available. (The woman character in "Hawk" wrote to her Cherokee friend, but he had not "answered.") But one such breakthrough allows her to write "A Sense of Place"; and this poem endows her with images that know and name. A girl she once saw walk *out* of Lake Michigan, "her wet hair gleaming and her skin," helps her to contemplate the monarch butterflies that must make their long flight from the "North" to Mexico: "I don't know how they can make it so far." And, in the language of the "Christine" poem, insight about self can teach the displaced woman, at mid-life, to put on the beaded blouse of black silk, to recall in herself the wildness of an Aztec princess, to spin glittering before the mirror, to dance, *knowing* she "dances the fault."

SHIRLEY CLAY SCOTT holds a Ph.D. in English from Kent State University and she teaches at Western Michigan University. She has published on contemporary literature in *Mississippi Review*, *Great Lakes Review*, *Nimrod*, *Ironwood*, and other publications. Currently, she is finishing a degree in classics.

Interview with Judith Minty

BY KAREN CARLTON

Question: In looking over the body of your work, what have you observed about your journey as writer?

J.M.: Well, that first book, *Lake Songs and Other Fears*, seems to deal with the child emerging from the parent at the same time that she's tied to place, to *the* place.

Question: Is this a psychological or geographical place?

J.M.: Maybe it's both. I know that things like "drowning" and "death," things about "Mother" and "Earth" and "Lake Michigan" appear in that book. Water imagery occurs over and over. Nearly the first poem in *Lake Songs* says it: "Like home. I was a child again." And the final poem in that book has as its last line: "It is a long drive home."

Question: Do you see yourself staying with those themes of childhood and place in *Yellow Dog Journal*, which, I believe, is your next published book?

J.M.: I guess I do. But this time she's going "home" to the Yellow Dog River, where "nothing [has] changed," where she finds "the Yellow Dog barking home to [Lake] Superior." In the Spring section of the second book, when she returns to the Yellow Dog, she says, "Still here. Still here," as if maybe it wasn't going to be. Then, in the opening section of *In the Presence of Mothers*, she continues that theme: "Live here always if you can . . . There are so many here to love." At the end of the section she tells us, "I'm trying. Oh all of you, I am coming home." But by the end of that book, although there is still the motion to return, the theme begins to be coupled with sorrow, with a real awareness of loss.

Question: You keep calling the "I" of the poem "she." Is this because you want to distance yourself from the autobiographical?

J.M.: I do feel separate from that woman in the poem at the same time that I'm connected to her. It seems to me that all poetry emerges from the personal. But it also goes through something like a tunnel of water—the creative process. When that happens there's a blend of memory and imagination and the work is no longer limited to the autobiographical. I begin to know that person in a different way than I know myself.

Question: "Letters to the Snow Country," your new working manuscript, seems to take this persona in the direction of the wanderer.

J.M.: That's right. From the very first page she's walking. By the time that manuscript comes along, there's the sense that nothing is permanent, that everything has an ending, that things change, that you can't go back. But she keeps on trying to re-define "home." In that manuscript, in one poem, "The Gray Whale," she's really talking about the whales, yet she means herself when she says "no one warned me about this." And there's the four-part "A Sense of Place" that appears in this anthology. In it, when she refers to the monarch butterflies' migration to Mexico, she says, "I don't know how they can make it so far." I do think there is hope for her, though it comes very late in the manuscript. By the end of "A Sense of Place," she begins to make a connection. She begins to see that no matter where you are, you're linked with the earth. And I think that's the realization she has been struggling toward in this manuscript. Maybe it has been her preoccupation since the first book, because there has been that awareness and investigation of migration, of splitting the self, of duality, ever since the beginning.

Question: So you see your earlier work as not only returning to your personal origins, but going even farther back to ancestral and archetypal realms. In that process, looking back and forth between what is your everyday home and your deeper home—the home of the spirit—you move to a third place which suggests you've got all of that inside you and now you are ready to go anywhere.

J.M.: I hope so, because otherwise. . . . You see, what *was* does not remain. The "child" is gone, as she discovers in *Yellow Dog*. The father that she really misses is the lost father—he is beyond being the father that she remembers. This means that the child is lost also as the woman moves into maturity. But even though the historical, experiential sense of place that was the child's undergoes changes in reality, it remains in the memory as a permanent thing. Relatives die, relationships disintegrate, our children leave home and begin their own lives, things are lost. What is retained, however, is the energy of what happened during moments that were shared. This means that, in going to my father's old fishing camp—which I did, and *Yellow Dog Journal* evolved out of that—I shared the energy of whatever had transpired for him when he was there because he still holds that in his memory. So what I'm doing, in some way, is building on what he had, which makes energy a continuum. I'm thinking again of the last poems in the new manuscript. In them "she" realizes that nothing belongs to her, nothing is hers. All there can be then, if there isn't anything tangible, is shared experience.

Question: Which you record in words. That is a way of holding on and letting go at the same time?

J.M.: Perhaps. Let me tell you something that Joseph Campbell said at his 80th birthday party in San Francisco last spring. He was commenting on the hero's journey and said this wonderful thing that

made perfect sense to me and enlarged on what I had been doing in some way: "All life is sorrowful," he said. We must "participate with joy in the sorrows of the world." I never thought I would have to make the journey from the inland sea of Michigan all this way to salt water.

Question: And is there joy in the sorrow of leaving your home and coming to the Pacific coast?

J.M.: I think I'm coming to an awareness that I must search within myself, that the connection with place is all-permeating, all-over. Or, that the wind really does find you. That we *are* the earth, in some way. Well, "she" finally discovers in the next to last poem in the new manuscript "Letters to the Snow Country," when it's raining all across the country, that you can be everywhere at the same time and that everywhere can be with you.

Question: Are you saying that living in California has given you a new perspective of Michigan and those old places?

J.M.: Yes, I think so. Because the past always colors the present. Zentatsu [zen master] Baker-Roshi says: "When the way is internalized, practice can be continued anywhere." It seems to me that we carry place with us. Just as it [Michigan] is my "heart" land, it is always in the heart. And I do speak of that place back there as Heartland. The Snow Country, The White Time—those names reverberate for me.

Question: Does that energy, then, only arise from the land?

J.M.: Strange that you should ask, because saying "whale" gives me the same energy as saying "the sea." How is it that sometimes we feel such a connection with the whale, who doesn't even walk on land. Or the bear, who does. Or the cat. Or the purple finch, who flies. There is something we as humans know—at the same time that we don't know it, and, if we bring ourselves close enough to the natural world, we almost remember it. It isn't so long ago that we forgot this either. It nearly comes back to us when we touch a tree— I've always thought I knew this. Why do myths of animals persist in our memories? Because they remind us of ourselves as we either are or wish to be, or might have been, or were but can't remember. And, see, that has nothing to do with geographical place. It's just all over.

Question: Is that why animals dominate your poetry?

J.M.: They're just there. It's not willful on my part. I've dreamed the bear for years, as I've dreamed other animals. They've been a part of my underworld life. They are me. I am them in that true sense of what emerges from the dream. Unfortunately, we don't remember that life all the time.

Question: Now I'm wondering about another new poem in this anthology, "Trying to Remember." Is this a new form for you? You have four alternate voices; it's structured like a song, a Bach toccata or fugue, for example. You have a male voice, a female voice, an old woman, and the earth. Four voices. According to Jungian and Native American world views, four is the number of wholeness. It seems to be a healing poem.

J.M.: It's a weird poem. I think they're all guides. There's the dark and the light of the two women who are approaching middle age. One wears the dark shawl and one catches sun in a crystal by her window, so two aspects of self are represented. And then, there's the sexuality of the male.

Question: I'm also interested in how the lines get shorter. It's as if the closer you get to this thing you are trying to remember, the less fluent you are.

J.M.: The tension is mounting.

Question: Yes, and the voice becomes oracular.

J.M.: The tension is really mounting. When it's read aloud, it's like she's *trying* to remember what her grandmother told her. Read aloud, there's a peak of intensity reached in the body and the voice.

Question: "Snow keeps falling, my tracks must be covered by now." There is that juxtaposition of losing the memory and the tremendous effort to retrieve it.

J.M.: That poem came to me because I was missing the old woman, the breath of her love on my arm. I couldn't remember what she had given me.

Question: But you keep on walking. The "Christine" poem summarizes in a wonderful and humorous way this notion of the wanderer. Even the ground you are walking on in that earthquake poem is shifting. And, "We must make adventure from these briefest shifts and passings." It's as if life is in-between one place and a second place, in the empty space between them.

J.M.: That's why I was so pleased and startled when I heard Joseph Campbell. If life is all-sorrowful, then we *have* to make adventure out of these movements. And there were also the literal facts of the "Christine" poem—Christine's passing through my life on her way to China.

Question: She's coming from your homeland, Michigan, to visit you in California, on her way to a still more remote place, China.

J.M.: Yes. She's going even further west, over the ocean.

Question: So there is all this movement, Christine, your relationship with her, the earth. . . . And you buy a blouse in the leap, during the shift.

J.M.: For me, that suggests that life just keeps going on. This whole process—this rite of passage from child to old crone—is just something we have to make an adventure out of. When my cousin died, my uncle said, "This is one thing I don't want to have to take." But we have to take this stuff and transform it into animals and Aztec goddesses. All of life is transformation. If we can go back and forth, into and out of the earth, into the sea to join with whales, then we've done a better job of getting through than we might have otherwise.

Question: I remember that in one section in *Letters to My Daughters* you say "Nothing remains as it was. If you know this, you can begin again with pure joy." How does that relate to transformation?

J.M.: I don't see the "I" in those *Letters* as me anymore. I see her more as archetypal mother. Even though it hurts to uproot, have your roots torn from the soil, you *can* begin again. Nothing stays the same. Just as it was with that fluid motion of "Christine," who travelled on after her brief stop in California. Campbell has that line: "I am it. It is in me." Of course, the myth is in us. The mythology we create we actually emerge from in some way. It is in us.

Question: Let's talk about your "Hawk" poem. It suggests the way you read signs in this world. Can you say anything about signs and the relationship of those signs to your poems? They seem to come to you from nature most often. The hawk feet, for example.

J.M.: That poem nearly wrote itself. It was one of those gifts that come at one sitting. I discovered the poem in the morning on my footstool where I'd left it the night before. I knew the hawk was a sign and I didn't leave the house after it came. I think we have to pay close attention to the natural world. It's like how some people talk about extra sensory perception. If the hawk had been an isolated experience in my life, I could doubt. Instead, there's the sense of paying attention to your dream. Which means that the hawk must have come from the same place the dream came from.

Question: When I relate your consideration of signs to your new role as the wanderer, I come up with an American Indian rather than a European consciousness. I don't want to set them against each other, but do you feel that that kind of consciousness enjoys a new dominance, or has it always been very strong in you?

J.M.: If anything, I'm losing it. I *am* part Mohawk, but I live within the dominant culture. So I have to be very careful all the time to keep that consciousness. I have to keep myself tuned. The last time I was up at the Yellow Dog I spoke with a friend afterwards who said, "You can't stay away

from the woods too long. You lose your touch for it." He may be right. If you stay locked up in a city or in academia, or any environment that takes from you—or even a bad relationship with another person, then your openness, your receptivity, begins to atrophy. When I feel that happening to me, I immediately get to water. I always have. That's one reason why the Great Lakes have been important to me. That's why the Pacific Ocean is important now. Or the Eel River in California. Or, of course, the Yellow Dog River in the UP [upper peninsula] of Michigan. It's important to know that that water was upstream, going over that big rock a few minutes ago. And now it's passing over this sandy spot. And soon it'll slip around that bend. There is a constant motion to water, as there is to the unconscious. It always revitalizes me.

KAREN CARLTON is an assistant Professor at Humboldt State University where she teaches Children's Literature, Adolescent Literature, and Writing. She has co-authored a *Handbook for Teaching Writing* published by the California State Department of Education and is currently conducting research on the uses of the unconscious in various modes of writing.

Editor's Note: Poems that appear in Judith Minty's published books are noted by source where discussed in the Critical Response and interview below. Those that have no source noted are from her new working manuscript, "Letters from the Snow Country;" many of these quoted poems appear in this anthology. A list of Minty's published books appears in our Biography.

Judith Minty: Biographical Notes

BY HELEN COLLIER

JUDITH MINTY IS a poet who has spent most of her life in Michigan. Both the Indian history and the mixed blood of immigrants peopling the land and building the cities are her beginnings. Judith is one of two children born into a middle class family recently risen from the working class in Detroit, Michigan. Her mother came from an English/Irish/American Indian family. Judith did not know that her maternal grandfather was a Mohawk until she was in her early teens. Her father, child of Finnish emigrants, was raised in the Upper Peninsula of Michigan, and he was determined to share his love of the North Woods with his family. Judith grew up with one foot in each of the worlds of her environment —the urban and the natural.

She spent the school year in Detroit, absorbing the culture of the arts—symphonies, dance performances, art exhibits, and libraries, and her summers in the North Woods of Michigan camping with her family in an area laden with Indian folklore/history and the pleasures of the outdoors. These two worlds were later to be melded into the artistic clarity of her poetry and its recurrent images of natural symbols (lakes, animals, Indian legends). Midwesterners often recognize in her work the everyday events and rituals in their own lives, the clear and white world created by a winter's storm, the dramatic changes of the seasons, and the presence, in history and legends, of Indians. Her poems give a physical sense of life in the Midwest.

While attending the Detroit public schools, Judith received recognition for her poetry in city-wide contests. In her late teens, a shifting of focus occurred as it does to so many women. The sense of "being what other people thought I should be" became so forceful she stopped writing poetry. She finished high school and entered Michigan State University, where she met and married Edgar Minty.

Together they moved to Ithaca, New York, where she graduated with a major in speech from Ithaca College. She and her husband subsequently returned to western Michigan where they raised two daughters and a son. Back in her own world, she began once again to write poetry and, in this new cycle of life, set about rediscovering her roots and exploring the North Woods of her childhood. Several summers were spent with the family living on a sailboat traveling the Great Lakes, the Georgian Bay, and the North Channel of Canada.

Judith returned to school and received her MA in English from Western Michigan University in 1973, the same year her first book, *Lake Songs and Other Fears*, received the United States Award of the International Poetry Forum. She has since published three other volumes of poetry, *Yellow Dog Journal* (1979), *Letters to My Daughters* (1980), and *In the Presence of Mothers* (1981). Numerous awards have been conferred upon her over the ensuing years, including the Eunice Tietjens Memorial award from *Poetry* magazine, the John Atherton Fellowship in Poetry to Bread Loaf, three residencies at Yaddo, and two Creative Artists Grants from the Michigan Council for the Arts. Funds from the latter have made possible the writing of her new working manuscript from which the poems used in this anthology are taken. A high degree of involvement in the arts in Michigan has included her roles as a participant for six years in the Michigan Council for the Arts Creative Writing Project, as a member of the Literature Advisory Panel of Michigan, and as Poet-in-the-

Prison at Muskegon Correctional Facility. Her poetry has appeared in many journals, including *The Atlantic Monthly* and *The New Yorker*, and in numerous anthologies, including *The Generation of 2000* and *Fifty Contemporary Poets*. Her most recent poetry manuscript, *Letters to the Snow Country*, is nearly completed and she is currently working on some short prose and a novel, *The White Time*.

Judith began teaching in the early seventies at Grand Valley State College, Interlochen Center for the Arts, and Central Michigan University. As the need to make a living grew, she became, like many poets of her generation, a wanderer, and traveled further and further away from her home, teaching at Syracuse University, the University of California at Santa Cruz, the University of Oregon, and Humboldt State University, where she is presently. Judith spends summers in a one-room house she and her husband built in the Michigan countryside which she describes as being on "a meadow-mound near a wooded cliff that overlooks Lake Michigan." As in her childhood, she returns to live on the land she cherishes and senses with her Mohawk ancestors that "I've belonged to those places for longer than my lifetime."

HELEN V. COLLIER, psychologist, author, educator, private practitioner, and consultant/trainer lived and worked in the Midwest until her recent move to Reno. She is the author of two books and many articles relating to the psychology of women. She currently teaches part-time at The University of Nevada, Reno, consults in both the public and private sector, and writes.

Country Road in October

The willow, still green,
keeps this white house chaste.
But oh, that saffron cottage.

    Cattails exploded,
    their dignity in tatters.

All the corn stalks point east.

    Red-tailed hawk
    drifting
    over what runs to hide
    in the barren field.

They'll be the last to go,
those chrysanthemums
bordering that driveway.

    This passage makes the chest ache.
    It's orange
    that hurts the most.

Apples dragging down the branches.
In the wagon, pumpkins.

    Even the *Daily News* box,
    yellow on its green stem.

I am amber
driving under the maples.

    The whole woods
    in holy color.

Breathing in the Woods

New snow, and I follow
the dim path through woods, sink
into silence. Meadow vole, squirrel,
snowshoe hare, fox:
my tracks walk next to theirs.
If it still falls tonight, by dawn
none of us have travelled here.

Indian Summer

Oh dragonfly, come to rest on my sleeve,
let's stay by this pond all afternoon:
you sunning on the wool of my sweater,
me lying on these feathery leaves.

Hawk

Dead hawk outside my bedroom window,
even the cats won't touch it.
I laid low for three days,
didn't leave the house,
and wrote my Cherokee friend.
He hasn't answered, the hawk's
been waiting. Today I took

the tail feathers and feet.
I feel worst about the feet,
hanging from the backporch beam—
fists clenched, claws like my own hand
holding the knife. I knew
when the other one flew over, keening,
he wouldn't recognize her like that.

Six Poems for Nine Crows

(after a painting by S. Krause in Philip Booth's apartment)

So.   April.   The crows in possession. PHILIP BOOTH

September now.
Only a breath of summer remains.
Uprooted, I stand at this eastern window
and watch sparrows drift from the maple
like brown leaves. I own nothing here,
the eye clear in new air.

Owl feather, finch petal, jay leaf,
flicker branch, pheasant stem:
feathers dropped in passage. Now I
plant them near his painting of crows in a field.
          One flaps his wings
          at a newcomer, beak open
          and shrilly warning. Another
          stands guard. The rest
          tend to the harvest.
These silent relics bloom
in their vases, each vein
of color defined, barbs
still poised to the flight.

Wherever we live, those we care about
find us and we wait for their letters.
They glide from post office to mailbox like
          homing pigeons,
the heart inside pulsing *peace, strength, friend.*

Now this news about rifles and chain saws
ripping Mohawk trees, about SWAT teams,

about women hiding in their houses, this plea
        to help
a stubborn elder who tried to save the trees *

makes my hands heavy.
600 miles west of here, and north,
are Chippewa woods. I'm a fool to imagine
no one has timbered that land since I left it.

        "Philip's tree."
        There, I've named it, the maple
        outside my bedroom window. I know it
        belongs to itself and I'm only a renter here,
        still he's told me the pleasure it's given
        so these words are for him:

        In this gale wind, far from the sea, your tree
        flaps its wings and turns wild.
        It means to lift up, soar back to its mother, back
        to the shade, the dark seed of before.
        I witness it all from your window,
        the wind calls through a thin crack.
        Even this paper flutters.

The station begun, though I'd meant to wait
a month for the earth's shell to form.
First a gossipy jay, then a grackle in mourning.
Now today, a convention of sparrows.
The whole balcony flickers brown. They feed
like horses at a trough, queue up on the railing for turns.
The thinkers take the floor and spilled seed,
beaks opening, closing, to the glory of food.

Last week, driving in the country, the sun barely risen,
I passed a farmer in overalls, bucket heavy at his side.
(He is crossing to his sheep. They nearly dance
at his coming, black faces nudging each other by the fence.)
We all tremble for something—the hand
to reach into the slop-pail, a letter,
the telephone to ring—our morning nourishment.

        *A near-violent dispute, involving
        questions of trespassing and
        sovereign rights, between Indians
        of the Akwesasne territory and
        the New York State government, was
        barely averted in the fall of 1979.

This place belongs to others. Stretching out
in these rooms, I sense the skin of their lives.
Walls don't keep secrets.
Each breath that seeps from our lungs
leaves a thread clinging to plaster or fabric,
a chorus of whispers humming.
The monstrous shadow rises and falls without
        the body
and we long for them to join again.
In this half-light, dark wings
burst open, the maple scratches at the window.

Trying to Remember

  A note from my friend on this morning of the first snowfall. Slow waxing in letters
exchanged, tones and contours spelled into words. Each envelope holds a mirror of feeling: two
women naked in each other's eyes.

*

  A month ago, close talk with this man I love, over cheese and wine at the kitchen table.
Drifting to food after languorous hours of hands fluttering, spiralling cries. We are lonely already.
We want to fly back to the body.

*

  She carries the dark side of the moon under her shawl. I catch sun in a crystal by my window.
We approach middle age together. Our words spin over trees, trill in strands, a sparrow's song.
Between us, we create another woman.

*

  Our fingers meet on the knife handle. Embarrassment at the collision, hands leaping away.
We try to come together with words, but his coyote eyes glitter, a wolf rises up through my
bones.

*

  She writes what her grandmother said: If you wash your face in the first snow, you will have a
beautiful complexion. Letters or books, something to hold in the hand. Her words are always
a gift.

*

  This good bread. We tear off chunks to eat with our cheese. He swirls wine in his mouth
before swallowing it. Grandmother said we must honor bread, he tells me. You must kiss it before
you eat it.

*

  Summer afternoon, my grandmother. Perhaps I am four or five. I am sitting on her lap. She is
humming, I think. It is hot and we have nothing to do, no chores, no one to play with. We want
and we do not want something.

*

Walking in the woods, first snow sifting through pines, white puffs of breath, leaves under my feet slightly muffled. The ground disappears, a veil shudders over the land.

*

She speaks of fire burning as her sons grow past her. I say my childhood ran away when I turned my back for a moment. She is pleased with this transformation. We change, she writes.

*

Ferns along the path are still green, though they are growing white skins. The weight of the snow bows the stems to the ground. It is cold and the fronds do not move when I pass.

*

When I sat on her lap, her fingers spun over my arm, her fingers traced lacy patterns on my skin. We were both half-asleep. She was humming, I think. The breath of her love on my arm.

*

The ferns, bent from such a little snow. A fallen birch across the path, the sound of my walking muffled.

*

His hands burn, set me trembling. The room whispers and sighs with our caring.

*

I was so close to her heart then, her fingers pulsing over my arm.

*

Snow touches my cheeks, my eyelids. The birch lies on top of the snow.

*

We are waking, she says. We have only been hibernating.

*

We must honor it. His hand holds the bread to his lips.

*

Snow keeps falling. My tracks must be covered by now.

*

I am trying to remember what my grandmother told me.

Christine, on Her Way to China: An Earthquake Poem

"Buy that blouse," she whispered,
the earth already moving, though we didn't know it yet.
We walked over from the car, the blouse
expensive, pulling us to the window.
We walked rich and daring, with that thrust to our hips.

The gold beads were electric; she was my friend.
The night before, when I confessed my sins,
we'd both wept for what might have been—
the dreams that never rose, the lost father of the child in us.
"Buy it," she said in her throaty Austrian way.

She'd just come from snow country to gape at fuchsias,
Scotch broom and poppies by the roadside,
to northern California, where everything grows big and wet and lush.
She'd come from barren white, a nine-month winter,
to trees in leaf and rivers shimmering like snakeskins.

I saw bolts of lightning explode from the black silk;
I felt something break, a sunburst;
I heard a rustle, the crack and fall of timber.
"Aztec goddesses in temples," said Christine.
"Will you take a charge card?" I asked the saleswoman.

The plates were sliding then, the brain exposed,
a flash and spark, granite rasping granite.
The jolt came then, the earth in motion.
Buildings swayed, chimneys fell, the TV talk was rock and grind and rumble.
I spun glittering before the mirror and knew we danced the fault.

Christine is flying now to China.
My earthquake blouse gleams from the open closet.
Someone told me once how he'd been standing in a valley,
felt the tremble, and watched the fields roll like ocean waves.
I thought, even then, how we are planted here,
how ordinary our lives are, how we must
make adventure from these briefest shifts and passings.

A Sense of Place

I

I recall that California yard full of caged birds
we used to drive past on our way to the ocean
and the parrot shop at the Santa Cruz Mall, alive
with exotic feathers—we all dressed in colors then—
that woman in the red cape who wandered Mission Blvd.,
street musicians in Guatemalan shirts,
flower shops with tubs of roses by the curb.
Now I'm in snow country, still thinking
of pink and yellow buildings, of persimmons
in the market, and rhododendrons flopping off their stems.
Here, these Eastern woods have just shrugged off winter
and the trees are full of brown birds,
bright voices hiding in the branches.

II

Summers ago in Leland, I watched a swimmer
walk out of Lake Michigan, her wet hair gleaming

and her skin, with its coat of oil,
glittering in the sun. Behind her, blue
and stretching into the sky, the water sparkled.
Everything shone, even crystals of sand around our blanket.
That was the month of butterflies, hundreds
of monarchs on their way to Mexico.
I don't know how they can make it so far.
Once, in California, I walked
through the eucalyptus grove at night
and heard the whisper of their wings while they slept.

III

When the bear came to me, I already knew
that trees walk at night, that the river speaks
and the wind knows everything.
It was October, evening at the Yellow Dog. I was
reading near the stove, trying to keep warm, trying
to ignore some mice building a nest on the shelf.
Maybe he was watching all week, maybe
he just saw my light. I don't know.
At first I thought his bawling and crying
were embers in the stove, then a cow,
but those woods were never farmland.
I turned down the lamp and ran to the window.
There was only my own reflection in the light from the fire.

IV

Just weeks ago I sat on the bank
of the Smith River, up near the Oregon border.
I was mourning snow then, dreaming white hills
and wishing cold wind in the face.
Now, I'm across the country and ice
has just let loose this pond. It's May,
bass shiver up from the mud and new leaves
reflect on the water's skin. I feel lucky
they've found me, whoever they are
that flow with the water, float on the wind.
At this moment, now, midges and darters skim the surface
and the bass break in circles to take them.

Meeting My Father at the River

On this evening path from camp
to river's bend, shadows
roll over and lie down in hollows,
then rise from rotting stumps

to drift along the lowland.
They stalk my boots' dull thud, branches
opening, closing overhead.
The cabin's lamp, the glowing stove,
burn behind me now in memory.

At the river, my father
still stands in light.
This will be his last trip to these waters.
His arm lifts, his line wavers,
settles over the pool.
I have often dreamed this motion:
me watching from the bank, him casting,
the whir of reel, the bend and dip of rod and arm.
Now a small trout rises to the fly.

He calls, "I got one, Judy!"
It surfaces, flickering in wetness.
He is pleased I am here to witness
and leans with grace in hip boots
for the ritual of netting,
stepping sure as a young man again.
"Good one," I cry, and wave.
He wades slowly out of sight
around the bend, creel bumping at his side.
I keep watch over the dark pool.

Walking

Walking, shoving my chin deep into the coat's collar, curling my hand around dustballs in the
    pocket,

walking past the house, the thermometer pointing its finger at freezing, past the old woman in the
    bandana and her wheat-colored stacks of pine needles,

past the giant pine I once crawled under to hide, now bending to touch a frosted cone hurled down,

past the row of cedars that guard the mouth of these woods, blue spruce with sagging branches,
    then scrub oak, scaring two partridge out of the brush,

walking, kicking maple leaves into the sound of fire, past a log blooming with polypores, past the
    pond that holds in its memory bass below, birch leaning over their mirror,

walking over moss, sinking into sponge, damp odor rising when the surface cracks, past the gray,
    ghostly beech, around mud not yet marked by a paw,

walking, cracking the air with a snap of twigs, out of light through the inner forest where branches hold hands and gleam in the silence, where dark marries day,

walking past the barbed holly, bluejay shouting warning, toward the clearing where firs groan and creak against the hair of the wind,

letting / the will / go

walking, my breath steaming, inviting the poem to rise up from these gnarled roots through the soles of my boots, my feet, the trunk of my body, my heart, to step onto this white page before the first snowfall.

Contributors' Notes

CAROL J. BARRETT, with a doctorate in clinical psychology, has an impressive list of published papers on such subjects as widowhood, gerontology, and women's psychology. Nevertheless, she's a poet as well with many published poems in *Nimrod*, *Kansas Quarterly*, and *Primavera*, to name a few. Working with Anita Skeen, her co-poet in *Woman Poet—The Midwest*, she recently blended poetry and psychology in a study of widowhood, published in *Signs*. Also with Skeen, she has completed an anthology of poetry on widowhood.

THERESE BECKER says she's lived life backwards: married, raised three children, and had a sales career before she turned to writing. Her poetry has appeared in *Poetry Now*, *The Midwest Poetry Review*, *Greenriver Review*, and others. Hand in hand with poetry is her deep interest in photography. Her photos have been well published. This four-time scholarship winner to the Cranbrook Writers' Conference writes: "My passions are my children, animals and Aikido. I have so many loves and goals I must live to be very old."

MAUREEN BLOOMFIELD, an instructor of English at the University of Cincinnati, has published numerous poems since 1976, when her first two, "Sunday in Berkeley" and "Fairy Tale," appeared in *Southern Poetry Review*. Among her accomplishments are two awards for her criticism as a writer of art reviews and an associate editor position on *Dialogue*, an art journal. She received an Ohio Arts Council grant, in 1983, and the Critic's Purse Prize, in 1984. Her poetry manuscript, "Grisaille," is in circulation, under serious consideration.

ARDYTH BRADLEY, winner of the Judith Wax award to "a woman writer of unusual ability," lives in Libertyville, Illinois. She has published one collection of poems, *Inside the Bones Is Flesh* (Ithaca House, 1978) and has worked as a college English instructor, news reporter, research writer for the U.S. government, publicity writer, editor of two biology textbooks, wife, and mother of three children. Her poems, fiction, and criticism have appeared in many publications, such as *Shenandoah*, *Quarterly Review of Literature*, *Ironwood*, *Tendril*, and *Banyan Anthology 2*.

JILL BRECKENRIDGE's inventive one-day workshop on the psychology and process of writing is named "Confronting the Empty Page." Currently Jill works with businesses, government agencies, and individuals, designing and teaching programs in creativity and fluent writing. With the assistance of two State Arts Board grants and a Bush Foundation Fellowship, she is also completing a book of poetry and prose, "Civil Blood," about Civil War General John Cabell Breckinridge. Her earlier book, "Act of Faith," is "out and about."

ALICE DERRY, long a Midwesterner—who has traveled and lived in Germany, Italy, and much of Western Europe—currently teaches English at Peninsula College in Port Angeles, Washington. She studied at Rocky Mountain College, Die Freie Universitat in Berlin, American University, and Goddard, where she received her Master of Fine Arts in 1980. A major interest is her work on Rilke translations, one of which has appeared in *Ironwood*. Her poems have been published in many journals, the most recent appearing in *Southern Poetry Review*, *Poetry*, and *Prairie Schooner*.

LORENE ERICKSON, a writing instructor at Washtenaw Community College in Michigan, has been in the public education winner's circle twice: in 1977 she was named Michigan's Creative Writing Teacher of the Year and, in 1979, she received an award for Outstanding Livonia Public Schools Educator. She edited *Waiting for the Apples* (Sylvan, 1983), a student anthology. Her first book of original poetry was *Seasons of Small Purpose* (Grand River Press, 1980). Her newer collection, on themes about women, won the first prize in the 1982 Judith Siegel Pearson national competition.

EDITH FREUND has experience in several genres: journalism, fiction, and poetry. As a journalist, she won national recognition on a series about children with learning disabilities. Her short stories have appeared in literary and commercial magazines in the United States, Britain, and Australia; her poetry has appeared in such publications as *Rhino*, *Another Chicago Magazine*, *Spoon River Quarterly*, and *Overtures*. Her first novel, *Chicago Girls*, was published by Poseidon Press (Simon & Schuster, 1985).

PATRICIA HAMPL was born and raised in St. Paul, where she now teaches at The University of Minnesota. Her most recent book is *Resort and Other Poems*, (Houghton Mifflin, 1983). Her prose memoir, *A Romantic Education*, won the 1981 Houghton Mifflin Prize. It is the story of her Midwestern girlhood and her later travels to the homeland of her grandmother. Currently she is at work on a novel. One of Hampl's two librettos for composer Libby Larsen, *In a Winter Garden* (a choral work for Advent), is available on the Pro Arte Label.

PHEBE HANSON started writing at the age of eleven but says that only within the past decade has she thought of herself as a professional writer. Her poetry now appears in such publications as *Saturday's Women* and *Minnesota Poets*. She teaches at the Minneapolis College of Art and Design. Her impressive list of poetry readings, beginning in 1976, includes a five-summer stint with a traveling troupe of poets and musicians who gave readings "to people in parks, art centers, nursing homes, bars, churches, and sometimes cemeteries."

LINDA HASSELSTROM lives, works, and writes on a ranch in western South Dakota. Some days are for working cattle, cursing the weather and feed conditions; others are for writing, or attending to the business of her independent enterprise, Lame Johnny Press. Her first book of poems, *Caught by One Wing*, was recently printed in letterpress (Julie Holcombe Press, San Francisco). Her writing has appeared in such diverse publications as *Midwest Quarterly* and *Playboy*. She won a National Endowment for the Arts fellowship for poetry in 1984.

JEANINE HATHAWAY teaches English at Wichita State University in their Master of Fine Arts program. A first play written with Stephen Hathaway, *Tales, Fables, and Nonsense*, was performed by the University Touring Company. In 1980 she won the Seaton Award for her poems in *Kansas Quarterly*. In 1981 she received a Faculty Research Grant to study for a year at the Centre Jeanne D'Arc, Orleans, France. Her poems appear in many anthologies and in journals from East to West, such as *The Georgia Review*, *New Orleans Review*, and *Poetry Northwest*.

SUSAN HAUSER lives with her husband on the edge of a floating bog in northern Minnesota. She teaches, freelances, and directs training workshops and conferences on a college level. Since 1973 she has been the publisher-editor-printer of the Raspberry Press. Her poetry has appeared in such publications as *New Letters*, *New York Quarterly*, and *Sing Heavenly Muse*. She says she learned to call herself "poet" in 1973, when she was enrolled in a Master of Fine Arts writing program at Bowling Green State University, Ohio.

PATRICIA HOOPER is blessed with honors that include finalist in the Yale Series of Younger Poets, five Hopwood Awards, the Bernice Ames Award, and an Elliott Fellowship from the University of Michigan. Her poems have appeared in such as *The Ohio Review*, *Poetry*, *Michigan Quarterly Review*, and *The Chicago Review*. *Other Lives*, her first book of poetry—a recent Yale Series finalist—was just published by Elizabeth Street Press, New York. She lives in Birmingham, Michigan, with her husband and two children.

JESSIE KACHMAR, with husband, child and a stack of poems, moved from Seattle to Chicago in the late fifties. She co-founded The Poetry Seminar with John Logan. She has taught high school and adult education classes, edited poetry journals, and been a long time teaching participant in two current workshops. In 1980, Jessie won The All Nations Poetry Contest. Jessie's first book, *Snow Quiet*, appeared in 1976. Her second, *Apertures to Anywhere* (1979), was written in collaboration with poets Helen Winter (who also appears in *Woman Poet—The Midwest*) and Phyllis Ford.

KARIN KANIA is an experienced psychiatric nurse. She has trained, supervised, and counselled mental health workers in all phases of therapeutic programs. Apart from her full time duties in the adolescent program at Kingwood Hospital in Ferndale, Michigan, she finds the time to be a prize winning poet, as the winner of The National Writers and *Writers Digest* poetry contests. In 1980 she was a guest at The International Poetry Conference, Cambridge, England. She is a member of the Detroit Women Writers and of the New York Poetry Forum.

FAYE KICKNOSWAY's drawings have won her as many awards as her poems; and they appear in all but one of her books. Her seventh book is *She Wears Him Fancy in Her Night Braid* (Toothpaste Press, 1983). Viking/Penguin will issue *They That Will Be Slain* later this year. Forthcoming in 1986 is *The Collected Poems* (Toothpaste Press). "My poems," she writes, "are what I see, what I hear, or imagine. . . . I am most interested in what is hidden and find information treacherous, drained of the events it summarizes and, therefore, a corpse."

CAROLINE KNOX's many recent achievements include earning a doctorate in creative writing, being a judge in Iowa's annual poetry contest, being an assistant librarian, and serving as an assistant editor for a theological journal. Her poems have appeared in *Poetry*, *The American Scholar*, *The Massachusetts Review*, and other journals. Her poetry collection, *The House Party* (University of Georgia Press), was a finalist in the 1982 National Poetry Series Competition. At the moment, she is trying her hand at short fiction.

MARGOT KRIEL is a jack of all literary trades. She is a literary critic, playwright, recipient of five important awards for her poetry. She has taught drama to college students and writing to hospitalized patients, adolescents in treatment for drug abuse, the mentally retarded, and college freshmen. Her recent major focus is developing a course for The University of Minnesota on women in the arts. Kriel grew up in the South, arriving in Minnesota in the late sixties. Recent poems have appeared in *Iowa Review*, *Milkweed*, and *Chronicle*.

MARGO LAGATTUTA's fine arts studies at Pratt Institute tie her to the visual as well as the literary arts. She teaches writing at the Paint Creek Center for the Arts in Michigan and is also a lecturer in poetry at some local colleges, high schools, and elementary schools. Prior to becoming assistant director there, she won two scholarships to the Cranbrook Writers' Conference. Some recent poems appear in *Passages North*. In 1983 she was nominated for a Pushcart Prize, and State Street Press released *Diversion Road*, her first book of poems.

JUDY LITTLE is a pure Midwesterner. She was born in Kansas, received her Ph.D. at the University of Nebraska, now lives in Illinois. She teaches Modern British Fiction, Women in Literature, and Creative Writing at Southern Illinois University. Her essays on Virginia Woolf, Margaret Drabble, and The Female Imagination appear in journals here and abroad. The University of Nebraska Press published *Keats as a Narrative Poet* (1975) and *Comedy and the Woman Writer* (1983). *Prairie Schooner* first published her poems. Since, she has self-published three poetry books.

JANIS LULL designs computer-assisted courses—including ones for the PLATO project, writes poetry, and teaches a variety of English and American literature courses, spanning from Shakespeare and the 17th century to contemporary poetry, at Case-Western Reserve University in Cleveland, Ohio. She received a Ph.D. from The University of Minnesota in 1983. Her poetry has appeared in such journals as *Epoch*, *Poetry Northwest*, and *Lake Street Review*; an essay in *Lewis Carroll: A Celebration*. She also free-lances as a copywriter and editor.

NAOMI LONG MADGETT became a published poet at age 11 when a poem she wrote appeared in a New Jersey newspaper; her first collection of poems was published six years later. An English teacher for more than 12 years in Detroit's public schools, she introduced an Afro-American literature course, received a distinguished teacher award, and was the first recipient of the Mott Fellowship in English. Recently, she retired from teaching at Eastern Michigan University to devote full time to the Lotus Press, which specializes in works by young black writers.

NANCY MCCLEERY is one of those lucky hybrids: a literary and visual artist. In addition to writing poetry, she makes prints, paper, and letterpress books. She's taken a second residence in Anchorage, Alaska, where she is a poet-in-residence at the Visual Arts Center. Her chapbook is *Night Muse* (Uintah Press, 1981); her poems have appeared in numerous magazines and journals. She also is a librettist for the Nebraska composer Robert Walters. Nebraska, she writes, is still home for her. Twice a year she "hops back to teach and give readings."

KAY MURPHY is both a poet and psychologist with graduate degrees and teaching experience in the two fields. She teaches fiction and poetry workshops for children and adults in dozens of communities in Illinois and, since 1978, has been on the faculty of Danville Community College. In 1980 she received an M.F.A. from Goddard. For five years, Murphy served on the Writers-in-Residence Program in Illinois. Her numerous poems have been accepted by such publications as *Spoon River Quarterly*, *Tendril*, and the *Seneca Review*.

KATHLEEN NORRIS lives in South Dakota, 125 miles from the nearest bookstore. She has written three books of poems; manages a family ranch, Leaves of Grass; and works for the North Dakota Artists-in-Residence program. She writes that she has read at arts councils, festivals, libraries, and museums in almost every community between New York City and Bismarck, North Dakota. She was the subject of a TV documentary on "Prairie Poets." *The Middle of the World* (University of Pittsburgh, 1981) is her most recent poetry book.

PAMELA PAINTER writes fiction and non-fiction as well as poetry. Besides teaching a writing workshop with the Harvard Extension Program, she is founder and an editor of *Storyquarterly* and former editor of *Canto*, both national literary magazines. Her recent poetry has appeared in *Literary Review*; her short stories in *Ploughshares* and *Threepenny*. She is the co-author of one novel, *Lucky to Be Alive* (Simon & Schuster), and two non-fiction books,

The Big Steal (Houghton Mifflin) and *The Divorce Handbook* (Random House).

MIRIAM PEDERSON taught English and has been poet-in-residence in six high schools in St. Paul and Grand Rapids. She is also the former project director of The Writer's Center of the Race Street Gallery. While raising two children, she continues to write, publish, and give poetry readings. She went back to college in 1981 and last year received her M.F.A. in creative writing at Western Michigan University. Her poems appear in many publications, including *Passages North* and *Primavera*. She has been a judge in poetry contests throughout the State of Michigan.

ALANE ROLLINGS' list of achievements is lengthy: a poet whose works have appeared in numerous publications; a book reviewer and literary critic for two Chicago daily newspapers; a former fashion designer; and a former producer of a University of Chicago public affairs television program. She also holds a Master's degree in Far Eastern languages and civilizations and is fluent in Chinese languages. Her poems have appeared in such as *Carleton Miscellany* and *Carolina Quarterly*. Her first poetry book is *Transparent Landscapes* (Raccoon Books, 1984).

PAULETTE ROESKE, a poet with a first degree black belt in Tae Kwon Do, has taught English at College of Lake County in Illinois for more than 15 years. Her poems have appeared in, among others, *Poetry*, *The American Poetry Anthology*, and the *Anthology of American Verse*. The award-winning poet's most recent honor was first place in the New Poetry Broadsides Competition. Her first manuscript, "Breathing Under Water," was a recent finalist at Wesleyan University Press. A chapbook, "The Legend of Annie Palmer," is just completed.

ALICE RYERSON, mother of four children, is a poet, psychologist, anthropologist, and the dedicated founder of The Educators for Social Responsibility. After retiring as a school psychologist, she worked on archeological digs. In 1976, she founded, directed, and became Chair One of Ragdale Foundation, a residential colony for artists and writers. Her poetry books are *Excavation* (Kelsey Street Press, 1980) and, last year, *Matrimonial Picnic* (self-published). She won the Illinois Arts Council Award for the best poem published in 1984.

JANET BEELER SHAW began winning awards for her poetry and short stories when she was in college, and, more recently, for her novel. Her short story "A Day for Fishing" was in the *Prize Stories of 1950: The O'Henry Awards*. Numerous poems by this mother of three have appeared in such as *Esquire* and *The American Poetry Review*. She has published two poetry books, *How to Walk on Water* and *Dowry* (The 1978 Devins Award winner), and a recent collection of short stories, *Some of the Things I Did Not Do* (University of Illinois Press).

MAXINE SILVERMAN is a native of Sedalia, Missouri, who now works in Manhattan. Since October 1983, she is the director of Special Projects at Sarah Lawrence College, a position involving programming for the arts, public relations, and fund-raising. She served as an editor of the important *Saturday Women* (1982) anthology. Her poetry has been published as a chapbook, *Survival Song* (Sunbury Press), and in anthologies such as *Pushcart Prize III: The Best of the Small Presses* and *Voices within the Ark: The Modern Jewish Poets*.

ANITA SKEEN has published more than 100 poems in many magazines: *Nimrod*, *Kansas Quarterly*, and *Prairie Schooner*, to name a few, and in six anthologies, including *I Hear My Sisters Saying* and *30 Kansas Poets*. She has three completed manuscripts—collections of prose poems, poetry about relationships with women, and an anthology of poetry on widowhood she co-edited with Carol Barrett, the co-author, with Skeen, of a poem in *Woman Poet— The Midwest*. She teaches creative writing and women's studies at Wichita State University.

GLORIA STILL writes short fiction as well as poetry. She gives innovative poetry readings accompanied by music and dance. Her honors include The Young Talent Award for Poetry from the University of Indiana Writers' Conference, a scholarship to study with Galway Kinnell, a National Endowment for the Arts fellowship, and many others. She has organized workshops and forums, taught French and English, edited journals, and produced plays. In 1980 she published *Serving Blood: New Poems by French Women*, a bilingual anthology.

MARY TRIMBLE is a screenwriter as well as a poet, with screenplays on American Playhouse, a nationwide PBS production. She free-lances both as a television writer and researcher. Her film production credits include *Who Am I This Time*, *Nicholas Nickleby . . .*, *A Matter of Principle*, and *The Roommates*. Her first poetry book, *The Woman at the Foot of the Mountain* (Black Cat Bone Press) was published in 1980. She currently teaches in an Illinois Artists-in-Residence program while working on a new book of poems and a screenplay.

CARY WATERMAN is a transplanted Easterner now living in Minnesota. She is the winner of many distinguished prizes and grants, including a Pushcart nomination for three successive years and two Bush Foundation Fellowships. She spent 1984 on leave from the Upward Bound Program at Mankato State University to be a resident at the Tyrone Guthrie Centre in Ireland. Two of her three books are *The Salamander Migration and Other Poems* (1980) and *Dark Lights the Tiger's Tail* (1981). She is now working on a book of poems about Calamity Jane.

HELEN WINTER's years between 15 and 19 were spent in a tuberculosis sanitarium where she wrote a poem every day. During that time, her frequent use of her Webster's dictionary earned her the nickname "Webby." Without a high school diploma, she passed the entrance examinations at the University of Chicago, where she took courses in English. With two other poets (see our Notes on Jessie Kachmar), she published a book of poems, *Apertures to Anywhere* (Harper Square Press). Her poems have appeared in such journals as *Massachusetts Review* and *Chicago Review*.

Gift Orders

Please enter a ☐ 1 volume ☐ 2 volume
☐ 4 volume (complete set) gift order sent to:

Recipient _____

Address _____

_____

City _____

State _____ Zip _____

Recipient _____

Address _____

_____

City _____

State _____ Zip _____

A Gift
to you for

from

Woman Poet
P.O. Box 60550
Reno, Nevada
89506

Recipient _____

Address _____

_____

City _____

State _____ Zip _____

Gift Book Subscriptions

Recipients will receive the below (left) gift an-
nouncement signed by you; gift orders begin with
the first volume in the series (*The West*), unless requested otherwise.

Collectors' Copies: Hard Cover Limited Editions:
$16.95 plus $1.50 handling.
Soft Cover Regular Editions: Individuals $8.50 each
plus $1.50 handling, Institutions $11.00 each.

Two volume orders, for example, *The West* and *The
East*: Soft Cover—Individuals $16.00, Students
$14.00, Institutions $20.00. Hard Cover—$32.00.
(*Countries other than U.S.A., Canada, and Mexico,
add $3.00 a volume.*)

Set of four regional volumes, beginning with the in-
augural volume unless requested otherwise: Soft
Cover—Individuals $30.00, Students $27.00, Institutions $38.00. Hard Cover—$60.00.
(*Countries other than U.S.A., Canada, and Mexico,
add $3.00 a volume.*)

Please enter my order for myself.

I want _____

Total enclosed: $ _____ Date: _____

Name _____

Address _____

_____

City _____ State _____ Zip _____

Mail with your check or purchase order to *Woman
Poet*, Women-in-Literature, Incorporated, P.O. Box
60550, Reno, Nevada, 89506.